Jewelry

Marshall Cavendish London & New York

Edited by Sue Simmons

Published by
Marshall Cavendish Books Limited
58, Old Compton Street
London W1V 5PA

© Marshall Cavendish Limited 1974,
1975, 1976, 1977, 1978

This material was first published by
Marshall Cavendish Limited in the
publications *Encyclopaedia of Crafts,
Golden Hands Monthly* and *Crafts Weekly*

First printed 1978

Printed in Great Britain
ISBN 0 85685 333 X

Above: The wealth of materials available for making jewelry means that a wide variety of necklace, or on a smaller scale, bracelet designs can be worked.

Introduction

Jewelry making is one of the simplest and most fascinating of all crafts. The wide range of skills and variety of materials available to produce individual pieces means that, with a little imagination, an almost infinite number of really original designs can be worked.

Jewelry explores many of the possibilities of working jewelry pieces in the home. Whether your taste is for ornate dress jewelry or you prefer the more natural effect of seeds and shells used as beads, the techniques and materials are explained in easy-to-follow terms and illustrated in detail. Each section is devoted to one material, and the skills necessary to work it, and is designed to enable you to master the basics before going onto the more advanced projects and eventually designing your own pieces.

The materials vary from the orthodox to the imaginative and are selected so that you will need the minimum of equipment. New materials, such as self-hardening clay and cold enamel, are included so that you can now work clay necklaces and imitate the exquisite finish of enamelling without incurring the expense of a kiln. Many materials can simply be found while on holiday – pebbles can be polished, shells segmented and painted and feathers dyed to provide unique and delightful jewelry pieces. And, by using your eyes and imagination, everyday objects such as forks, pasta and tissue paper, can all be transformed into striking jewelry.

Fully illustrated throughout, with step-by-step diagrams to help you work each project, *Jewelry* provides all the information you require to make and design your own individual jewelry pieces.

Contents

Bead jewelry

Simple bead threading

The first steps in jewelry making are some of the most exciting. With the basic threading and knotting techniques, and an understanding of the right threads and fastenings, a dazzling treasure chest of necklace designs opens up. It also means you can go through your jewelry box and either mend or restyle existing pieces.

Making your own necklaces is great fun and the results are, of course, unique and very personal – and also surprisingly inexpensive. But before you get carried away with enthusiasm, it's well worth learning the appropriate thread, closure and knotting technique for a well-finished, durable result. There's nothing more irritating than an unknotted thread breaking and showering beads all over the floor!

Most modern necklaces fall into one of three categories. First there is classic simplicity, reminiscent of traditional ropes of pearls à la

Opposite: A selection from the wide range of beads available in shops and stores. From top left: heart-shaped, small-shaped and pear-shaped glass beads; blue glass lustre; Venetian mosaic; bugle beads; lamb's eye; rocailles (in box); turquoise rotelles; sequins; brass nuts and washers; gilt half cups; brass pipe olives; Indian gilt beads; fish vertebra; white tubular rotelles; ostrich egg discs; brown ceramic bead and a mixture of wooden beads.
Right: Many natural objects can also be threaded. This necklace is made up of date stones, coffee beans, seeds and bone segments.

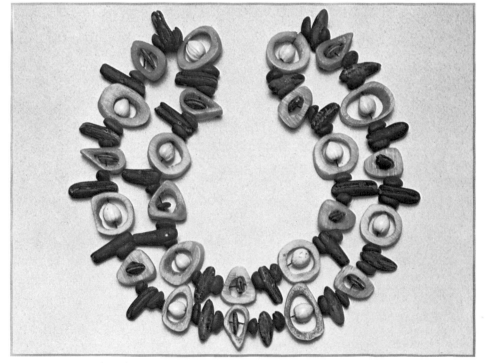

1920s, perhaps knotted at the bosom. Then there is the delicate look which uses sequins, tiny glass beads and mother-of-pearl. Thirdly, there is an important trend towards the primitive, with hand-made, slightly uneven shapes, marvellously contrasting textures and bold use of colour. Basic back-to-nature materials are much in evidence – wood, bamboo, metals, shells, clay, glass, bone and even nuts, seeds, dried berries, animal and fish teeth, pieces of bone, scraps of leather and pieces of driftwood.

Where to find beads

Craft shops are an Aladdin's cave for the jewelry maker, selling multi-coloured beads as tiny as hundreds-and-thousands or as large as a ping-pong ball; wooden balls, natural or dyed, and polished in a rainbow assortment of colours and just as many sizes; textured, rough cut stones; bamboo and ceramics cut into macaroni shapes; glass beads – plain, iridescent or marbled, and discs made from clay, wood or – expensive but utterly ravishing – mother-of-pearl.

Some unusual glass beads which are inexpensive and easily obtainable are:

'Eye' beads which are hand-made in the Middle East and are believed to ward off the evil eye.

Rotelles are beads with large holes and look like round beads that have been patted flat.

Rocailles are the smallest of beads and come in a multitude of colours.

Bugle beads, thin and tubular, are often used in elaborate embroidery.

You can buy buttons and sequins from haberdashers [notions counters] and brass nuts and washers from ironmongers or hardware shops. Don't forget junk stalls and sales as secondhand clothes can provide antique buttons quite cheaply, and special stones or a pretty clasp can be salvaged from broken necklace pieces.

Threads

The thread must be fine enough to pass through the holes of your beads, but sufficiently strong to carry their weight.

Synthetic sewing thread is fine but tough – ideal for tiny beads. It comes in a wide range of colours and is best used in conjunction with a beading needle.

Linen carpet thread is thicker and stronger. It, too, comes in a good range of colours and is useful for slightly larger glass or ceramic beads and small light wooden beads.

Fishing nylon 0.2mm (5lb breaking strength) from sporting goods shops has the advantage of being almost transparent, but is slippery

Right: A variety of necklace designs using nuts and washers. Threads for these designs must be strong and pliable, yet narrow enough to pass through the smallest diameter centre hole of the nuts and washers. The amount of nuts needed can easily be calculated by laying a selection of nuts on a ruler and measuring how many fit to the centimeter or inch. Reading from the top, the necklaces are numbered from one to five. Choker 1 is made of 8 large and 30 medium brass nuts and 12 large and 20 medium brass washers strung on fine roller blind cord. To prevent movement after stringing, tie a single knot at the end of the nuts and finish the cord ends by knotting or dipping into clear nail polish. Choker 2 uses twin corded flat cord linked, as shown in the photograph, around 18 × 8mm ($\frac{5}{16}$) steel washers. Choker 3 is simply 160 collared washers strung on nylon cord and finished with a single knot. Necklace 4 uses nuts and washers of varying sizes, achieving its balance by alternating brass with steel. Because the necklace is heavy, you will need to use four lengths of knitting cotton thread and, to prevent chaffing, make the part which passes around the neck with velvet ribbon. Loop this around the knotted ends of the four threading cords and sew neatly. Choker 5 uses three sizes of steel washers and one size of hexagonal steel nuts.

and can be difficult to knot. Threading a needle and knotting are made easier if you first flatten the end of the nylon.

Foxtail is a strong, knitted metal thread useful for heavy, opaque beads such as marbled Venetian glass.

Shirring elastic can be bought in various thicknesses, usually only

in black or white, and is particularly useful for bracelets without clasps, designed to be slipped over the hand. It is best used with beads with large holes so that the large knots can be hidden by pushing right inside a bead hole.

Leather is strong, chic and excellent for large items. Rounded rather than flat thongs are easier to thread, but sometimes more difficult to obtain. They can be found dyed in a good range of colours and are rigid enough to thread without the aid of a needle.

Other useful yarns are bead silk, dental floss (obtainable from pharmacists), strong twist thread, thin cords and macramé twine.

Threading

Long thin beading needles are useful for threading beads with small holes, but needles of different gauges can be used as long as the eye will pass through the bead.

Some threads are stiff enough to be passed through a bead without a needle and other threads can be dipped in glue or twisted with soap to stiffen the ends.

Bead knotting

You may want to use knots for a variety of reasons: to space out the beads as part of a design; to space them out in order to make them go further; or to secure each bead, so that if the necklace should break, all the beads will not slide off.

1–4 The type of knot used in jewelry making differs in relation to the size of the bead hole and the thickness of thread.
1. Overhand knot worked with double thread.
2. Double overhand knot.
3. A bead knot.
4. Small bead threaded each side of a large one.
5–7 Different forms of closure without using bought fastenings.
5. A tie closure.
6. A pull closure.
7. A button loop closure.

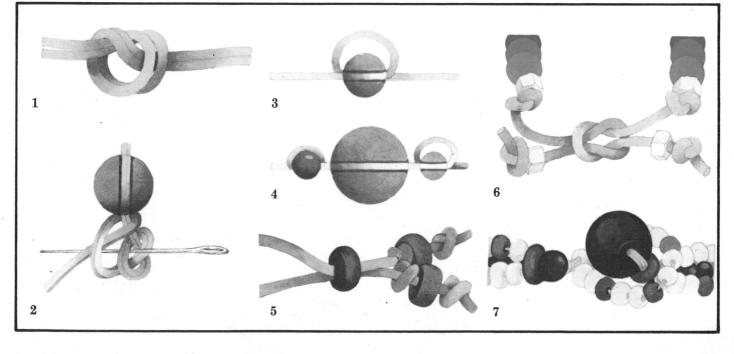

The knotting method depends on the relationship between the bead hole and the thickness of the thread.

Overhand knot If you tie an overhand knot, ensure that it is large enough to prevent the bead from sliding over it. Unfortunately, you will only be able to find this out by trial and error.

Double overhand knot If you wish to knot the beads very closely, as for pearls, you will find it easier to make a fairly loose, double overhand knot, then ease it up to the bead with a needle, and pull it tight up against the bead.

Bead knot If the thread is fine enough to pass through a small bead twice, you can string a small bead on each side of a larger one, passing the thread twice through the smaller beads.

Choosing a fastening

Rounded leather lends itself to the simplest fastenings of all – tie closure and pull closure, which need no clasps.

Tie closure Check that the beads are in the centre of the leather, then fasten each end by making an overhand knot after the first and last bead. Leave 15cm (6in) then make another overhand knot, thread a single small bead, make a final knot and cut the leather. If the bead fits tightly the second knot can be omitted as illustrated.

Pull closure When all the necklace beads are in position, thread both ends of the thong through a single, tightly fitting bead or washer. Leave 15cm (6in), then finish off each thong separately with overhand knots and a bead as described above.

Button loop closures These can be used on necklaces threaded onto synthetic or linen carpet thread. Finish off one end of the necklace with a well secured, large bead, and the other end with a series of smaller beads threaded to form a loop. Make sure the large bead will fit through this loop, then pass your thread through the loop beads a second time and secure by threading back and

Right: Metal fastenings. From top left to right: Gilt screw clasp; gilt bracelet clasp (open); gilt hook and bar; nickel bracelet clasp (closed); gilt box clasp; large nickel bolt ring and jump ring; two small bolt rings and split rings.
Far right: Means of attaching bought metal fastenings.
1. Starting off with a bolt ring.
2. Finishing off with a split ring.

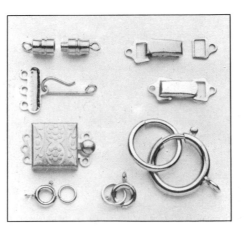

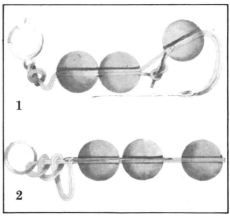

knotting through several inches of the necklace itself. Alternatively, glue the ends of the threads before passing them through the last bead. The glue will adhere to the inside of the bead and hold it securely out of sight. Use this method for finishing off thread ends.

Metal fastenings (or findings) Jewelers and craft shops supply traditional necklace clasps, bolt rings and screw rings. They may also stock closures commonly used on watch straps, and hook and eye fastenings in various sizes and different metals. Some findings have perforated surfaces so that smaller beads can be stitched on.

Attaching findings

Bolt ring Thread the yarn through the clasp eye. Tie an overhand knot with double thread next to the clasp. Tie the ends with a knot and snip neatly, so that, as beads are threaded, one of the beads hides the knot.

Split ring Finish off by looping the thread around the split ring, knotting and then re-threading the ends back through the last couple of beads.

Box clasps For extra strength and a neat attachment, first loop the thread through one end of the clasp, then pass both ends of the thread through your needle and string the beads onto the double thread. After the necklace or bracelet is finished, take the thread ends under the tongue and the back of the clasp, and then take them up through the last two beads.

Sequins with their lovely mother-of-pearl effect, can be used to make attractive and unusual chokers and necklaces. Sequins are either sold loose in boxes or threaded on string. The ones on strings are more convenient and less expensive. There are 1000 sequins on a string and a string measures roughly 22cm (8½) long. So, to make a choker-type necklace, you will need at least 2 strings. Working from this you can estimate how many strings of different colours you need to buy. For threading use fine gauge nylon fishing line as the stiffness of this thread means you will not require a needle.

Finish off with either a jump ring and clasp or, for long necklaces, simply knot the ends together with a reef knot.

Threaded bead necklaces

Opposite: Brass washer and bead necklace.

If you are going on to designing your own jewelry pieces, it is worthwhile giving a lot of thought before you actually start to which threads and fastenings are best both from the design aspect and, probably more important, for strength and durability of the finished piece.

With a knowledge of the basic techniques described in the previous chapter, a whole range of necklace and, on a smaller scale, bracelet designs can be worked. Here we give eight simple projects, each using a different combination of materials, to illustrate the variety of effects that can be achieved.

Washers and beads necklace

Thread a white bead at one end of the leather thong and tie an overhand knot at either side to secure.

Leave 15cm (6in) free for tying the necklace. Thread a black oval bead. This should fit tightly onto the thong but if it slips, simply tie an overhand knot to hold the bead in place.

Thread a white bead and 6 brass washers, then continue threading as in the illustration, placing the large brass olive, flanked by the small brass olives, in the centre.

When the last black bead is threaded, finish off to match the other end.

Two strand necklace

This necklace uses a gilt box fastening which is simple to fit. Attach one length of thread to the outside hole on the clasp, following the instructions given previously for attaching a bolt ring fastening.

Thread the beads as follows: brass bead, brass cup, 10mm ($\frac{3}{8}$in) lemon bead, brass cup, brass bead, brass cup, 6mm ($\frac{1}{4}$in) lime bead. After the 7th wooden bead (4th lemon, 3rd lime), thread a 10mm ($\frac{3}{8}$in) lime bead, then a 12mm ($\frac{1}{2}$in) lemon. Continue threading, alternating the colours as before.

After the 11th large lime bead, thread the smaller beads as before. Fasten off in the outside hole of the other half of the clasp.

For the inner strand, attach thread to the inner hole of the clasp.

Washers and beads

You will need:
0.75m (28in) of round leather thonging.
60 × 12mm ($\frac{1}{2}$in) diameter brass washers.
4 × 18mm ($\frac{3}{4}$in) round glass beads (2 yellow, 2 green).
6 × 12mm ($\frac{1}{2}$in) round flat beads (orange).
22 × 6mm ($\frac{1}{4}$in) round beads (white).
2 × 12mm ($\frac{1}{2}$in) long oval beads (black).
2 × 3mm ($\frac{1}{8}$in) brass olives.
One 6mm ($\frac{1}{4}$in) brass olive.

Two strand necklace

You will need:
2 × 1.25m (4ft) lengths of linen thread.
Blunt needle.
Gilt box clasp with two or three attachments for thread.
12 × 6mm ($\frac{1}{4}$in) wooden beads (lime).
20 × 10mm ($\frac{1}{8}$in) wooden beads (lime).
16 × 10mm ($\frac{3}{8}$in) wooden beads (lemon).
18 × 12mm ($\frac{1}{2}$in) wooden beads (lemon).
132 brass cups.
68 small brass or gold beads.

Work as before but with 9 large lime and 8 large lemon beads in the centre. Fasten off in the inner hole of the other half of the clasp as described above.

Glass lustre necklace

Fasten one end of the thread firmly to the bolt ring of the fastener.
Thread as follows: brass cup, lustre bead, brass cup, brass bead, two brass cups, brass bead, brass cup, lustre bead.
Continue threading in this way until the end, then attach the split ring and fasten off the thread.

Glass necklace

This necklace, made of multi-coloured glass beads, is fairly long and will not therefore need a fastening.
Thread the beads and fasten off very firmly, poking the knot back inside the bead and threading any excess back through two or three beads.
These beads are expensive, so it is a good idea to make a knot between each one for safety.

Red, white and blue necklace

Fasten the thread firmly to the bolt ring of the fastener using an overhand knot.
Thread as follows: one white, one dark blue, one white, one red. Continue this sequence ending with one white, one dark blue, one white.
Attach split ring and fasten off thread by re-threading the ends back through the last couple of beads.

Beads and brass nuts

Making sure that the beads lie in the centre of the leather thonging, make a knot close to each end bead.
Leave 15cm (6in) free for tying, then make a firm knot, thread the last rotelle bead at each end of the thonging and finish off by knotting again.

Lamb's eye necklace

Thread 13 rotelles, one dark green bead, 3 rotelles, a lamb's eye, 3 rotelles and a dark green bead. Continue this pattern until the last green bead, then thread 13 rotelles.
Make sure the beads are in the centre of the thonging and knot close to each end bead. Leave 15cm (6in) free for tying, make a knot, thread the last rotelle at each end and knot again.

Glass lustre necklace
You will need: Gilt bolt ring with split ring.   1.5m (5ft) of linen thread (use double).   Blunt needle.   27 × 10mm ($\frac{3}{8}$in) glass lustre beads (blue).   106 brass half cups.   52 brass beads.
Glass necklace
You will need: 60cm (2ft) of foxtail or 1.25m (4ft) of bead silk or strong thread (double).   Blunt needle.   49 × 10mm ($\frac{3}{8}$in) Venetian mosaic beads.
Red, white and blue
You will need: Bolt ring with split ring.   1.25m (4ft) of thick linen thread (use double).   Blunt needle.   14 × 6mm ($\frac{1}{4}$in) tubes (red), 2.5cm (1in) long.   30 × 6mm ($\frac{1}{4}$in) rotelles (white).   15 × 6mm ($\frac{1}{4}$in) rotelles (dark blue).

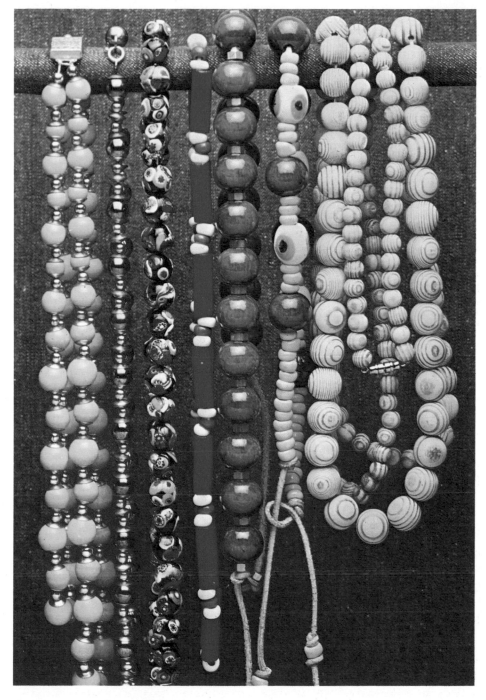

Beads and brass nuts
You will need : 1m (1yd) of natural, round leather thonging. 20 × 18mm ($\frac{3}{4}$in) shiny, large-holed wooden beads (dark green). 23 × 6mm ($\frac{1}{4}$in) brass nuts.
Lamb's eye necklace
You will need : 1m (1yd) natural, round leather thong. 6 × 18mm ($\frac{3}{4}$in) shiny, large-holed wooden beads (dark green). 58 × 6mm ($\frac{1}{4}$in) rotelles (light blue). 5 × 12mm ($\frac{1}{2}$in) lamb's eye beads.
Long wood necklace
You will need : 3.5m (11ft) linen thread (used double). Blunt needle. Nickel screw clasp. 80 × 6mm ($\frac{1}{4}$in) wood grain beads. 40 × 10mm ($\frac{3}{8}$in) wood grain beads. 25 × 16mm ($\frac{5}{8}$in) wood grain beads.

Long wood necklace

Attach the thread to the screw fastening and thread 40 × 10mm ($\frac{3}{8}$in), 25x16mm ($\frac{5}{8}$in), 20 × 10mm ($\frac{3}{8}$in) and 40 × 6mm ($\frac{1}{4}$in) beads. Attach to other half of fastening.

Rocaille designs

The simplest beads of all, tiny rocaille beads, threaded one after the other, rely on their colours for impact and yet their size means they can be modelled into small delicate shapes and patterns to give that individual touch to your jewelry.

There are several techniques to experiment with which are simple and straightforward to master, yet give a great variety of effects. You can experiment with any type of bead you like, but the tiny rocaille keep the flower shape best and have the delicately pretty look of embroidered daisies.

You'll probably find that a maximum of three colours gives the most attractive results. If you make long necklaces, they slip easily over the head and their pattern is not interrupted by a clasp. Make several to wear together with a matching bracelet. For threading, linen thread is strong and ideal for most beads. Tight neck chokers should be threaded onto shirring elastic.

Threading

Cut a length of thread or shirring elastic thread to the desired length, allowing an extra 12.5cm-15cm (5in-6in) for ease of working with the needle. In the case of a necklace, make sure that the length goes over the head easily before starting to thread the beads; it's extremely frustrating to have three-quarters of the necklace finished and then discover that it isn't going to be long enough.

Thread a needle and tie a double knot at one end of the thread. Pass the needle through a bead and slide the bead down to rest against the knot. Pass the thread through the knot to secure the bead and pull tightly. Then thread on selected beads and, at intervals, work one of the motifs given below.

Motifs

Triple bead motif After having threaded a number of main-colour beads, thread 3 contrasting ones. Pass the needle up through the first of the contrasting beads and draw up the thread tightly (fig.1). Continue threading beads as before.

Bead loop Make this in the same way as the triple bead motif but

---

Rocaille designs

You will need:
A selection of coloured rocaille beads.
Large sewing needle. (Make sure that it will pass comfortably through the holes in the beads being threaded.)
Linen thread or shirring elastic thread on which to thread the beads.
Glue or clear nail polish, for securing the ends of the thread.
Cushion pad or large, form pin cushion if you are using the double threading technique, given below.

Left: The tiny and versatile rocaille beads lend themselves to intricate and delicate designs ideal for making necklaces, bracelets and rings. A blending of two or three colours often gives the best results but a careful combination of brightly contrasting colours can often be used to great effect.

1. Working a triple bead loop. Having threaded a number of main-colour beads, thread three contrasting ones. Pass the needle through the first of the contrasting beads and draw up the thread tightly.

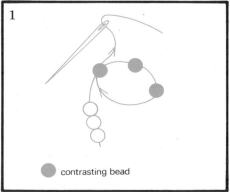

1

contrasting bead

add as many contrasting beads as you like to the loop before passing the needle through the first contrasting bead and pulling the thread tight (fig.2).

Daisy motif Thread 5 beads of one colour, followed by a bead of another shade. Pass the needle through the first bead (fig.3) and pull tightly. Thread 3 more beads of the main colour, then pass the needle through the bead on the other side of the contrasting one (fig.4). Pull the thread tightly to form the flower. The contrasting bead now lies in the centre of the circle formed by the 8-main-colour beads making an 8-petal flower.

Fastening off the ends

The ends of the thread must be finished very securely indeed and this is done by working a series of slip knots (sometimes called buttonhole stitches) between the beads.

With the needle still on the thread, pass it through the first few beads at the other end of the necklace. Make a firm slip knot. To do this, pass the needle around the thread between two beads, and take it through the loop thus formed (fig.5). Pull tightly. Pass the

2. Bead loop. This is made in the same way as the triple bead motif, but add as many contrasting beads as you like before passing the needle through the first contrasting bead and pulling the thread tight.

3, 4. Daisy motifs. These are a variation of the basic bead loop. To work, thread 5 beads of one colour, followed by a bead of another shade. Pass the needle through the first bead and pull tightly.

4. Thread 3 more beads of the main colour, then pass the needle through the bead on the other side of the contrasting one. Pull the thread tightly to form the flower.

5. Fastening off the ends,

6. Flower motifs threaded at intervals to form a daisy chain.

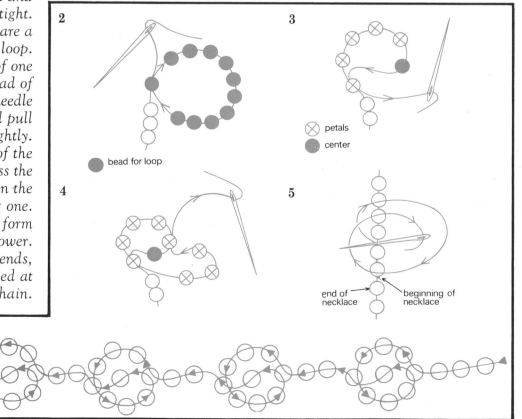

18

needle through a few more beads, then make a second slip knot. Work a third if the necklace is particularly long or heavy.

Finally, pass the needle through four more beads and then cut the thread. Dab a little clear glue or nail polish onto each knot as it is worked for additional strength.

Designs

Rocaille beads can be used for all kinds of jewelry. Below we give some of the finished designs along with their working instructions. You can either work these as given or incorporate them into designs of your own.

Multi-coloured bracelet This bracelet has eight strands, each 16cm (6¼in) long, and consists of 760 rocaille beads in a variety of colours. At the ends, the strands are tied together on a clasp after being threaded through a single rotelle bead.

Red and white multi-strand necklace This is made up with four strands, each 61cm (24in) long with 680 red and 680 white rocaille beads plus 152 small rotelles, one placed on each side of the 76 large coral rotelles.

White and blue necklace This design is made using two threads, each 91.5cm (36in) long. The white rocaille sections have two strands while the blue rotelles are threaded using both threads as one.

Each white strand has 40 beads joined by 12 blue rotelles – in all, 880 white beads and 132 blue.

Bead loops Two of the rings have four-bead loops while the red and white necklaces above and below have three- and five-bead loops respectively. To make to fit, there are 15 rocailles per 2.5cm (1in).

Red and yellow flowered necklace This design uses the daisy motif in groups of four with two white beads between each flower followed by white sections of about 80 rocaille beads each. Follow fig.6 or figs.3 and 4 for threading.

Black and white flower necklace This is made by repeating the daisy motif, each containing eight beads plus a gold centre. Four flower motifs equal 3cm (1¼in) in length.

Below: A few of the many effects that can be achieved using different colour combinations and different threading techniques with rocaille beads.
1. Bead loops.
2. Multi-coloured bracelet with eight strands.
3. Red and yellow flowered necklace.
4. Black and white flower necklace.
5. White and blue necklace.
6. Red and white multi-strand necklace.

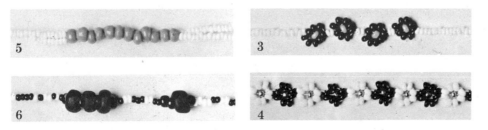

19

Bead mosaics

Beaded belt

You will need:
5mm (⅕in) matt-finished wooden beads– 280 black, 60 turquoise, 60 violet, 50 pink, 50 orange, 50 brown.
11.5m (12½yd) knitting cotton thread.
10 darning needles.
1 metal belt fastener.

Building up dense surfaces or 'fabrics' entirely of beads looks hopelessly complicated but is, in fact, as straightforward as stringing a single row once you have mastered the basic techniques of bead mosaics. Although these techniques are often used for large projects, such as bags and boleros, they can also be worked on a smaller scale to make attractive bracelets, belts and necklaces.

There are three basic methods of working bead mosaics and each can be quickly grasped by following the route of the thread in the following diagrams.

Working bead mosaics

Alternating bead method To make bead fabric in this way, simply thread one row of beads, fairly loosely, to the desired length. Then take the thread back through the last bead but one and every other bead in the first row, adding a new bead between each re-threading as shown (fig.1). You will find the bead fabric builds up quickly and easily.

Two cord technique Before you begin to work with this method tie the first bead to a secure working surface such as a chairback or polystyrene block.

Thread a needle onto each end of the cord you will use to string the beads. Pass one needle through the secured bead and draw the cord through until it is exactly half way through the bead and both needles are parallel.

Following fig.2, thread two beads (B and C), then pass both needles through the next bead (D) so that the cords cross. Continue working, repeating B and C, then D again. To tighten beads, pull both cords. To turn a corner, cross the cords through the bead on the

Below left: Belts can be threaded to any width and length using the multiple cord method.
1. Adding alternate beads builds a mosaic.
2. Making bead fabric using two cords.

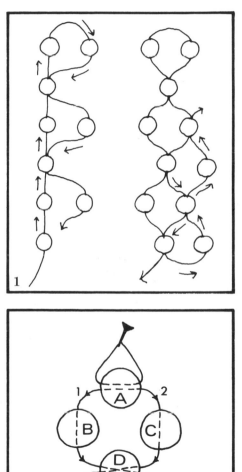

right side as shown (fig. 3).

Fig.4 shows how to work back up the length. This time the cords cross on the top bead.

Multiple cord technique This involves working with a row of cords, each of which has been folded in half and attached with a loop to a working surface. Figure 5 shows a belt buckle with a row of double cords, to illustrate the method of attaching the cords to the working surface.

Depending on the thickness of the cord, you can either thread the end of each strand onto a needle or stiffen it with wax.

The difference between the multiple cord technique and the other techniques is that in the multiple cord method all the beads are parallel. In the other mosaic patterns they are staggered. To begin, pass the two threads in each loop through a bead to make one row as shown (fig.6). Work two more rows in the same way, pushing the beads up the cords to the top.

Now thread one bead onto the first cord and pull the second cord across to the third one. Thread the next bead onto the second and third cords as shown (fig.6).

3. Turning corners with the two cord method.
4. Building up a two cord mosaic.
5. Multiple cord beadwork knots.
6. A finished length of multiple cording showing the direction of threads and the parallel structure of the design.

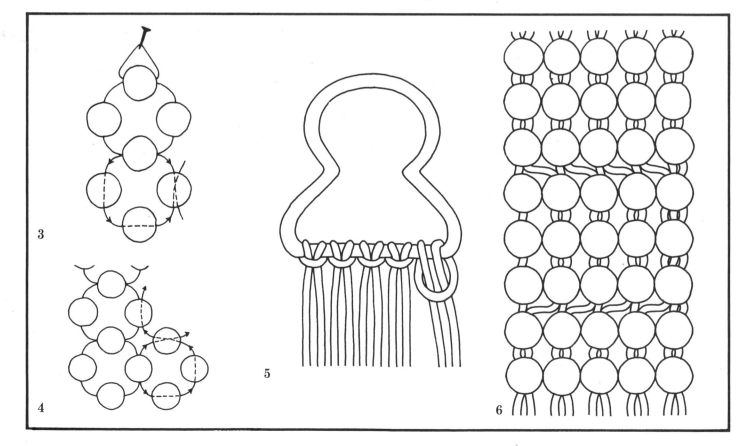

Likewise, pull the fourth cord across to the right, threading the next bead onto cords four and five, and so on. The last bead will have three cords through it and the first bead only one. Thread the next two rows as the first row except that the first and last beads have one and three cords through them respectively.

Thread the next row, pulling the cords to the left this time (reverse procedure from row four) so that the cords return to their original position. Continue as above, separating the cords after every third row.

When working mosaics with this method the cords can be separated after any number of groups of rows but, the smaller the groups, the stronger the fabric will be.

Beaded belt

The beaded belt in the photograph was made using the multiple cord technique, described above. Cords were pulled sideways after every third row.

Fig.7 gives the colour pattern and fig.5 shows the clasp used. The length of the belt illustrated is 62cm (24½in) excluding clasp. To

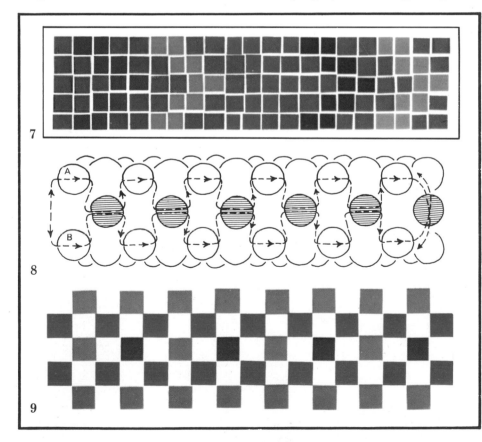

7. The colour chart for working the beaded belt.

8. Joining the ends of the bracelet. Using two needles, pass the thread through beads A and B, leaving an equal amount of thread on each side.
Using a beige bead, pass both needles through it in the same direction. Separate the threads and continue as with A and B, introducing a new bead at each junction.
To fasten off, work both threads down a short way on each side. Knot to the adjacent thread, trim off and secure with a dab of glue to prevent the knot unravelling.

9. Colour chart for working the mosaic bracelet, using the two cord method and elastic thread.

23

lengthen or shorten, remember each row is 5mm ($\frac{1}{5}$in) long and the repeat pattern is 12cm ($4\frac{3}{4}$in).

Work according to instructions for 'multiple cording technique', using 10 cords (5 lengths folded double). Thread the end of each cord with a darning needle and follow the colour chart (fig.7).

When you have worked through the repeat pattern start again – this time at the second row of the diagram.

At the end of the beadwork design work one row of black beads as in the very first row of the diagram.

To finish the belt, work a series of knots around the other half of the belt fastener and thread the spare lengths back through the beads to prevent the knots unravelling.

To make mosaic bracelet

The bracelet is worked with the two cord method and uses elastic thread, which makes a clasp unnecessary.

Follow the grid pattern (fig.9) to work the design.

To join the bracelet, insert the remaining beige beads, using figure 9.

To finish, knot the ends of the elastic thread firmly to adjacent cords and secure with glue.

Mosaic bracelet
You will need : 10mm ($\frac{2}{5}$in) shiny wooden beads: 33 beige, 26 orange, 6 brown. 1.8m (2yd) black round elastic thread. 2 tapestry needles.

Right: This mosaic bracelet is worked using the two-cord method with elastic thread so that a clasp is unnecessary. The matching bag shows how beads can be threaded into a mesh of any size using the easy mosaic method.

24

Bead weaving by hand

There are two types of bead weaving – on a loom and by hand. Bead weaving on a loom creates flat strips, bead weaving by hand creates a strip or circle of beads that will curve round a shape.

Weaving contours

The simplest type of hand bead weaving involves making long strips which can be used for necklaces or even edgings for collars and cuffs.

This method starts with a string of beads as long as you want the finished beadwork to be, and then a series of loops is attached to the beads, and to each other until the piece is finished (fig.1).

If the piece is the wrong length when finished, it can easily be shortened or lengthened by adding on or taking away from the initial string of beads. Many different patterns can be created by using different coloured beads and changing the zigzag pattern (fig.2).

The zigzag pattern created by the loops becomes larger towards the outside edge and this makes the curved contour which is suitable for such things as the curved edges of a collar, or to make the necklace shown here.

The necklace

This necklace fits around the neck and curves out gently to follow the neckline. It is made using the bead weaving method just described.

In the instructions the beads are described as: c=cream, w=wine red, o=burnt orange, y=yellow, b=rust brown, r=red.

The first row Thread the needle with a long double thread and rub it with beeswax to prevent it tangling. Tie a knot at the end of the thread.

Thread one c bead and pass the needle through the double thread between the knot and the bead and pull the thread tight (fig.3). Then thread enough c beads to make a rope long enough to fit comfortably around your neck. Pass needle back through the last bead but one and pull tight.

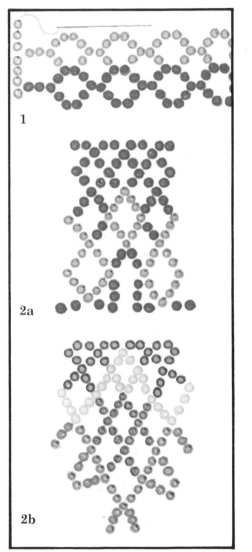

1. *Basic bead threading.*
2a, b. *Two repeat patterns showing how the shape and colours can be varied.*

25

The pattern The loops are attached after every third bead on the rope and connected to each other to form the zigzag pattern. Onto the same thread, thread 5w, 4o, 9y, 10b, 21r. Pass the needle back through the first r bead and pull firmly.

Thread 7y, and pass the needle through the first y and last o beads already strung (fig.5).

Continue by threading 3o and 3w beads and passing needle through the first 2w beads threaded.

Following fig.6, pass needle along 3c beads of rope and continue threading next series of loops attaching them to the first.

To renew a thread, fasten the old thread back into the necklace by making a series of slip knots. To do this make a circle with the thread, then pick up inside the circle the thread which lies between the thread you have just come out of and the thread you are going into (fig.7).

Pass the needle through two more beads and make another slip knot. Then pass the needle through two more beads and cut off the thread. Dab the slip knots with some colourless nail polish so that they stay in place.

Continue attaching loops to the necklace until you reach the end of the rope.

To finish Pass the thread through the last c bead of the necklace and then attach the fastener.

Finish off the thread by making a series of slip knots back into the necklace.

To complete the necklace, simply sew the remaining part of the

Right: Bead weaving by hand is ideal for making necklaces or collars as it creates a strip or circle of beads that will curve around a shape. This necklace fits around the neck, then curves out gently to follow the neckline.

fastener firmly to the other end of the necklace design. Using this basic construction, but changing the colour arrangement of the beads can produce many beautiful patterns.

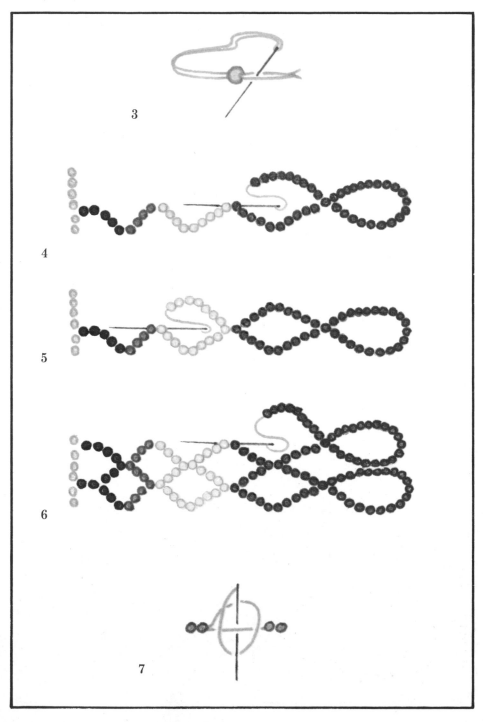

3. Securing the first bead on the chain.
4, 5, 6. Stages in the construction of the bead necklace.
7. Making a slip knot between two beads.

Bead weaving on a loom

Weaving beads on a loom is similar to fabric weaving. The warp threads (the ones going lengthwise) are stretched onto the loom and the weft (the threads going from side to side) are threaded in and out of the warp. One bead is caught up between each warp thread to produce flat strips of beadwork and the beads lying in parallel rows. On the finished work, none of the warp or weft threads are visible between the beads.

The loom

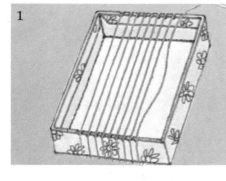

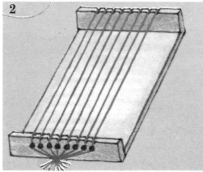

Bead weaving looms can be made at home from a cardboard box with cut notches or wood and nails (fig.1) and these are perfectly adequate for weaving small pieces of beadwork.

If you want to weave long pieces it is necessary to buy a loom which enables you to wind the work on as it progresses. There are two types available: a wooden loom and a metal loom. The metal loom has rollers at each end which enable you to wind the work backwards and forwards quite easily. On a wooden loom the work can be wound on, but not as easily as on a metal loom. The instructions given here apply to a metal loom.

Setting up Each warp thread should be 45cm (18in) longer than the

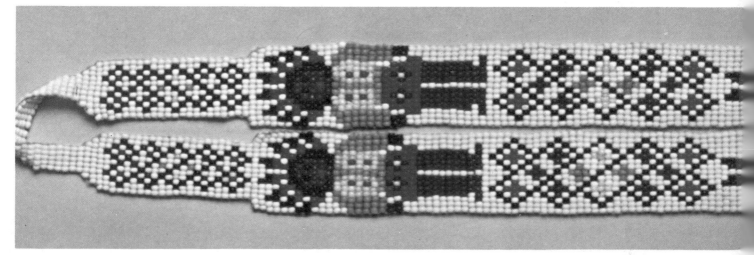

finished work is to be. The number of warp threads should be one more than the number of beads which will be on each row. A piece that is nine beads wide will need ten warp threads.

First the warp threads are placed side by side and joined together at each end with a knot. One end is secured in the rivet on one of the rollers, and the warp threads are wound onto this roller until the knot at that end can be attached to the roller at the other end.

The threads are then spaced out over the separator, one thread in each groove. The knot is secured to roller rivet.

The width of the bead loom obviously limits the width of the beadwork that can be made on the loom. The metal loom has separators for 35 threads which means that 34 beads is the maximum width that can be made. Many strips of 34 beads wide could be made and sewn together side by side to provide a wider strip. Very long pieces can be made by winding the work onto the rollers, and by joining strips end to end there is really no limit to how long a piece can be made. The warp on a home-made loom can be set up as in fig.1.

When the warp is on the loom, the weaving can start. A beading needle is threaded and the thread knotted to the outside warp thread on the left-hand side. The number of beads required for the first row is threaded onto the weft thread and passed underneath the warp threads.

With the other hand, one bead is pushed up between each warp thread and the needle is passed back through the beads, over the top of the warp threads, thereby securing them to the warp (fig.3).

To wind the work on as it progresses, the screw at the side of the roller is loosened and the roller turned. The warp does not have to be slotted into the separator again as the beadwork already woven will space the warp correctly.

Opposite: Simple bead weaving looms can be made at home.
1. Simple cardboard loom with notches.
2. Wood loom with nails.
3. Passing the needle around the end warp thread and back through the beads.
Bottom: Detailed photograph of the Indian necklace.

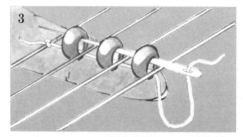

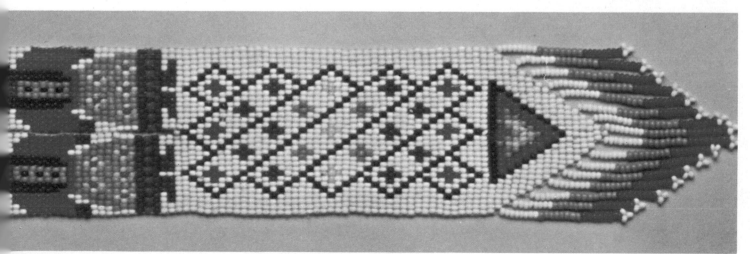

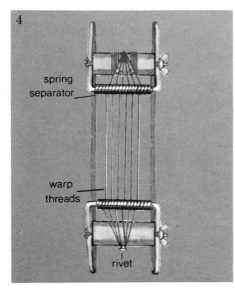

4

spring
separator

warp
threads

rivet

4. Details of a metal loom. These are ideal for working long pieces of bead work as they enable you to wind the work back and forth as desired.
Right: Metal loom with separators for warp thread and roller for winding work.

Indian necklace

You will need :
Beeswax.
Beading thread, made by manufacturers like Coats.
2 beading needles.
Bead loom.
Glass beads size 10 (about 1mm ($\frac{1}{16}$ in) diameter) in the following colours and amounts:
57gm (2oz) white.
28gm (1oz) black.
14gm ($\frac{1}{2}$oz) red.
14gm ($\frac{1}{2}$oz) dark blue.
14gm ($\frac{1}{2}$oz) yellow.
14gm ($\frac{1}{2}$oz) light blue.
14gm ($\frac{1}{2}$oz) brown.

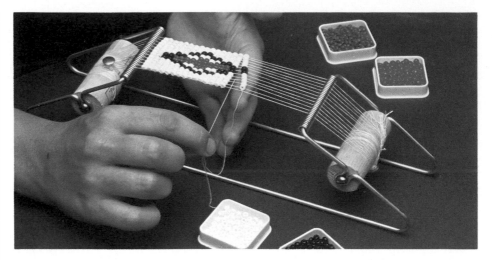

Indian necklace

Bead weaving is a traditional craft of the American Indians. This necklace is based on the colours and designs used by them for centuries to make jewelry and other decorative objects.

In the instructions w=white, r=red, b=dark blue.

Thread the loom with 32 warp threads 81cm (32in) long as explained earlier. Thread the needle with a long thread, double it and rub with beeswax. Tie it to the sixteenth warp thread from the left-hand side. This is where the weaving starts to create the V shape at the bottom of the necklace. (The fringe is made later.)

Following the photograph thread one w bead onto the warp thread. Pass the thread down between warp threads 15 and 16 and up between threads 17 and 18 (counting from the left-hand side). Push the w bead up between threads 16 and 17 and thread the needle through it.

Thread 3w beads, pass the needle down between threads 14 and 15 and up between threads 18 and 19, push the beads up between the warp threads and pass the needle back through them. Continue in this way following the pattern in the photograph.

Wind on the work when necessary. To divide the threads after row 59 has been worked, move 16 warp threads along the comb at the top which separates the warp threads and continue weaving up one section.

When you have finished one side, start the other side using a new weft thread tied to the 17th warp thread.

When the necklace narrows, move the surplus warp threads slightly away from the weaving by hooking over the spring separator and continue the pattern. The warp threads will later be fastened into the beadwork.

The fringe When you have completed the bead weaving, roll the beadwork back onto the top roller until the beginning of the necklace is sitting between the separators.

Cut the first warp thread as close to the knot as possible and thread it onto the needle. Thread 8w, 8b, 8r, 3w. Pass the needle back through 8r, 8b, 8w. Pass the needle through a few beads on row 15 and finish off with a slip knot.

Repeat this with each warp thread.

Finishing off There are two methods of joining up the two ends. The first method involves weaving each warp thread into the other side of the necklace and securing with slip knots. This gives a very neat reversible finish.

Ask someone to hold the two ends of the necklace together while you tie one warp thread from each side together to form a row of knots. Dab each row with colourless nail polish. Glue a piece of suede or felt to the row of knots to cover them up and strengthen the join.

Left: Woven bead necklaces based on traditional designs of the North American Indians.

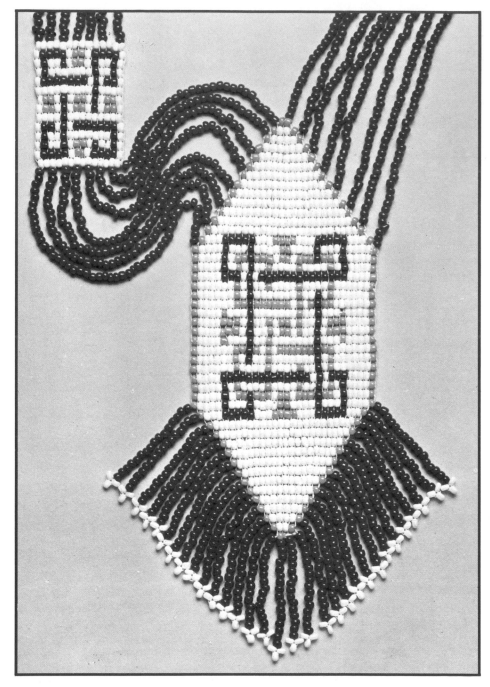

Right: The blue and white necklace. Work the design from this photograph by counting the beads and the rows.

Blue and white necklace

You will need :
Bead loom.
Beading needle.
Beeswax.
Beading thread, made by manufacturers like Coats.
Glass beads size 10 (about 1mm ($\frac{1}{16}$in) diameter) in the following colours and amounts:
85gm (3oz) dark blue.
28gm (1oz) white.
14gm ($\frac{1}{2}$oz) green.
14gm ($\frac{1}{2}$oz) light blue.

Blue and white necklace
This is made from three solid pieces of bead weaving held together with strings of beads.
In the instructions d=dark blue, g=green, w=white.

Thread the warp on the loom as described earlier. You will need 31 warp threads each 81cm (32in) long.

Wind 25cm (10in) of the warp threads onto the bottom roller before starting to weave – this will be used later for the fringing. Thread a needle with a long double thread, rub it with beeswax and tie to the 15th warp thread counting from the left-hand side.

For the point, thread 2g beads and push the needle down between the 14th space from the left and up through the 17th. Push the beads up between the warp threads and thread the needle back through them.

Thread one g bead and pass the needle down through the 14th space and up through the 13th space. Hold the bead between the 14th and 15th warp threads and pass the needle back through the bead. This bead is now the first on the second row.

Thread the remaining beads of the second row, i.e. 2w and 1g, and secure between the warp threads in the usual way, passing the needle through all four beads.

Continue weaving following the pattern shown in the photograph. Complete 32 rows.

To decrease for row 33, pass the needle back through the first g bead of row 32. Now move the outer warp threads slightly away from the main body of the work and weave as before on fewer warp threads. As fewer beads are threaded for each row the work will decrease on both sides.

Repeat this method for decreasing for each row.

When you have finished row 46, fasten off the thread in the row before by making slip knots.

Remove the top of the warp threads from the loom and onto each pair of warp threads starting from the left- or right-hand side thread d beads in the following order and amounts: 48, 44, 41, 39, 38, 34, 32, 30 (onto one warp thread), 30, 32, 34, 38, 39, 41, 44, 48. This makes sixteen ropes altogether.

Replace the warp onto the loom. Thread a needle and tie the thread to the 15th and 16th warp threads. Weave the square on the left of the necklace following the pattern. Use warp threads 15 and 16 as one.

Weave the square on the right-hand side on the remaining 15 warp threads.

The fringing

For the fringing roll the beadwork back onto the top roller until the end of the necklace is sitting between the separators. Release one warp thread at a time from the knot and thread onto this warp 16d and 3w beads. Pass the needle back through the 16d beads and fasten the thread by making a series of slip knots into the bead-work. Repeat this for each warp thread.

To finish off Remove the necklace from the loom, and on to each pair of warp threads put sufficient d beads for the required length. Tie the matching warp threads together and dab the knots with colourless nail polish.

Thread the ends through a few beads and trim.

Below: This tight-fitting, striking bracelet can be made on a warp of shirring elastic so that no fastening is needed.

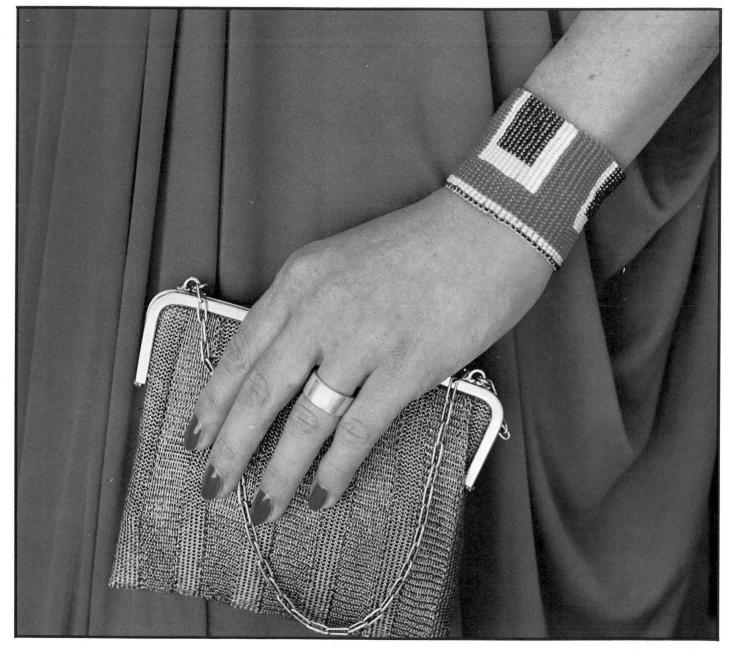

Beads and macramé

Macramé is the art of tying knots in string or yarn to produce a decorative design. With the addition of carefully selected beads, sandwiched between the knots, you will produce really beautiful results in no time at all.

Mounting strands

Cut strands of string equal to eight times the length of the finished article. The number of strands required depends on the width of the article. Cut one strand, the one that will be mounted on the far left-hand side, a little longer than the others. You can mount the strands directly onto a buckle or clasp if you like, or onto

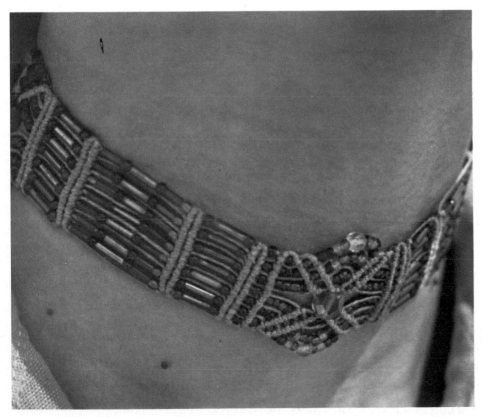

The combination of bright shiny beads and matt natural string, with their different textural qualities and contrasting colours, gives a really stunning effect to this choker.

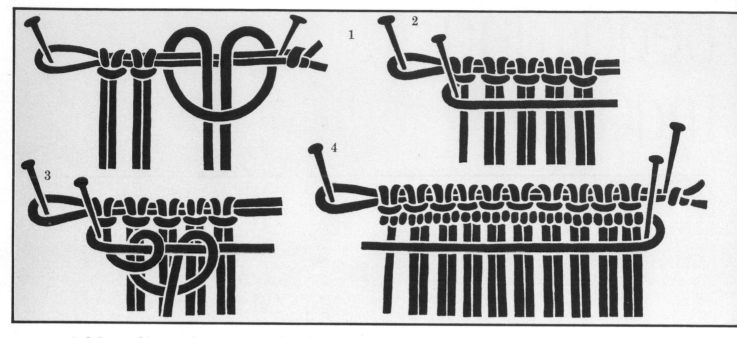

1. Mount the strands onto the knot bearer or leader, placing the long strand on the extreme left-hand side.

2. When working double-cording (half-hitching), position the extreme left-hand strand horizontally over all other strands and catch with a nail.

3. Bring the next strand up and over the horizontal strand from front to back, threading the end between the two loops so that the horizontal strand is caught between the two loops.

4. Having worked a complete row, fold the knot bearer or leader back over the other threads and secure the loop with a nail.

another length of string held down on the wooden plank at either end by a nail. This is called a knot bearer or leader. Fold all the strands (called knotting strands) in half and mount them onto the knot bearer (fig.1), placing the long strand on the extreme left hand side. The knots should be pulled tight so as to feel firm but not distorted and should sit side by side so that they are just touching each other.

Double cording [half-hitching]

This cording can be used both immediately after mounting the strands and as an integral part of the design. The cording has to be knotted around a knot bearer, which, in this case must be formed by the left-hand knotting strand as the cording is to be part of the overall pattern.

Take the extreme left-hand knotting strand and position it so that it lies horizontally over all the other strands pointing towards the right and catch the loop with a nail (fig.2). This row of cording is done by knotting from left to right. Bring the next knotting strand—the partner strand of the one lying across the top of the work—up and over the horizontal strand from front to back, threading the end between the two loops so that the horizontal strand is caught between the two loops (fig.3). Repeat with each strand in turn, working to the right. The horizontal thread or knot bearer must be held firmly each time that the other strands are looped around it. When you are working towards the right,

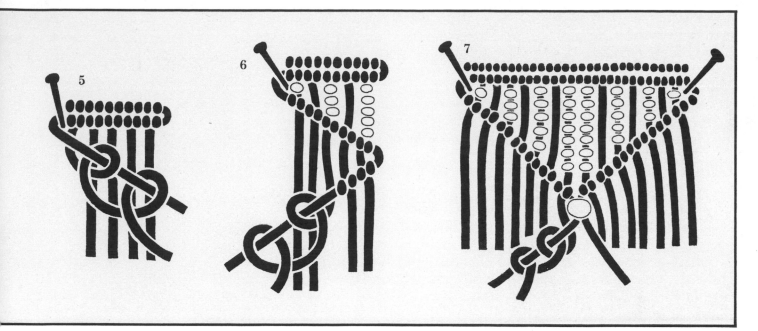

hold the knot bearer with your right hand and work the loops with your left hand.

When you have reached the far right-hand side and have worked an entire row of double cording [half-hitching], fold the knot bearer back over the other threads, again in a horizontal position and secure the loop with a nail (fig.4). Work a second row of double cording [half-hitching], this time working towards the left.

Threading on beads

Working from left to right: 1st strand: 1 round bead, 1 long bead, 1 round bead.

2nd strand: none. 3rd strand: as for 1st strand.

Continue in this way until you reach the end of the row. Block off the beads by working another row of double cording [half-hitching] as for the first row. Lay the first strand on the left horizontal across the other strands towards the right and catching the loop with a nail as before, and work a series of knots to sit just underneath the beads.

Diagonal motif

For this pattern, the knot bearer is positioned so that it lies diagonally over the other strands (fig.5). A row of double cording [half-hitching] knots is then worked, taking each strand in turn, and leaving a larger space each time between this and the last row of double cording [half-hitching] as you work. If threading on beads,

5. *To work the diagonal motif, position the knot bearer or leader diagonally over the other strands.*

6. *Thread on the beads in a diagonal design and fold the knot bearer or leader back over the threads and catch with a nail.*

7. *Work the cross motif, divide the strands into two equal groups and work both separately as for the diagonal motif, working both into the centre of the design. Having attached the bead as the centre of the design, continue to work a diagonal row of double-cording (half-hitching) working towards the outer edges of the design.*

make sure you thread them on so that the diagonal design is maintained e.g.

First strand: 1 bead   Second strand: none
3rd strand: 3 beads   Fourth strand: none
Fifth strand: 5 beads.

Continue in this way until you reach the end of the row. To work back to the left, fold the knot bearer back over thread, again in a diagonal position, and catch loop with a nail (fig.6).

Cross motif

Divide the number of strands into two equal groups. Lay the first strand on the left diagonally across the other strands to form a knot bearer. Thread beads on as for the diagonal motif and work a row of double cording [half-hitching]—again as for diagonal motif —until you reach the last strand on the left-hand group (fig.7). Similarly, work the second group of strands, working from right to left (fig.7.).

Thread the two diagonal knot bearers through a bead with a sufficiently large hole and cross them over.

Taking the diagonal knot bearer from the right-hand group, continue to work a diagonal row of double cording [half-hitching] towards the left (fig.7).

With the diagonal knot bearer from the left-hand group, continue to work a diagonal row of double cording [half-hitching] towards the right.

Finishing

After the last row of double cording [half-hitching], thread a small bead onto each strand, tie a firm knot just under the bead to hold it in place and cut off the string close to the knot. You can coat these first knots with a little transparent adhesive to ensure that they are secure.

Orange and black necklace

Lay two black 60cm (24in) strands and one black 180cm (72in) strand horizontally on a board and pin them securely in place.
For the centre section, mount two orange 90cm (36in) strands and

Above right: The orange necklace is a version of the black and orange one with extra cording on the side motifs and a plain centre.
Below right: This necklace combines beads with double cording, over-hand and flat knots.
Right: The ends are glued down and finished with a hook and eye fastening.

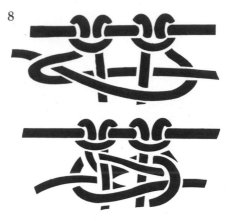

8

8. *Working a flat or square knot, the two centre cords are used as a core. Holding these taut, form a loop using the right-hand thread and pass the end under the centre core and over the left-hand thread. Bring the left-hand thread over the core and thread it through the loop from the front of the work. Pull up tightly. To complete, simply reverse the method.*

Orange and black necklace

You will need:
Two strands black, 60cm (24in) long.
Two strands black, 180cm (72in) long.
Eight strands black, 90cm (36in) long.
Two strands orange, 90cm (36in) long.
Ten strands orange, 60cm (24in) long.
46 yellow glass rotelle beads.
1 long orange wooden bead.
Clear glue.
Hook and eye.

four black 90cm (36in) strands each side.
For the side sections, mount five orange 60cm (24in) strands on each side.
Lay the remaining 180cm (72in) black strand parallel to the mounting knots. Make double cording [half-hitching] knots over it with each strand.

Side sections With the centre two strands as knot bearers leading to left and right, make double cording [half-hitching] knots over them. Make a flat [square] knot with the centre four strands.
Thread three beads on the centre two strands. Make an overhand knot and finish each strand with overhand knots. Finish all the other strands with overhand knots.

Centre section With the centre two strands as knot bearers leading to left and right, make double cording [half-hitching] knots over them.
Counting from the centre, thread a bead on the second and every alternate strand on both sides.
Use the centre strands as knot bearers and make double cording [half-hitching] knots over them to left and right as above.
Tie a flat [square] knot with the centre four strands. Thread a yellow bead over two strands and the long orange bead over one strand.
Make double cording [half-hitching] knots over the knot bearer just used, working towards the centre and including the strand that was by-passed by the orange bead.
Counting from the centre, thread a bead on the second and every alternate strand, which means that there will be five on the left and four on the right.
Using the outer orange strand as knot bearer, make double cording [half-hitching] knots over it towards the centre.
On the centre two strands, thread a bead, make a flat [square] knot with four strands, and repeat three times more.
Finish by threading beads on the two outside strands and tying overhand knots. Tie overhand knots on the two centre strands.
Finish the four strands each side with beads, and secure with overhand knots. Tie overhand knots with the remaining strands.
Trim the ends fairly close to the knots. The decoration is now complete.

To make the neckband Work fifteen flat [square] knots each side of the decoration, or until the neckband is the required length. Trim the strands and fray the ends.
Dab a little glue on the ends and press them to the wrong side of the neckband.
When the glue is dry, sew the hook and eye to the wrong side of the neckband. The necklace is now complete.

Jewelry from clay

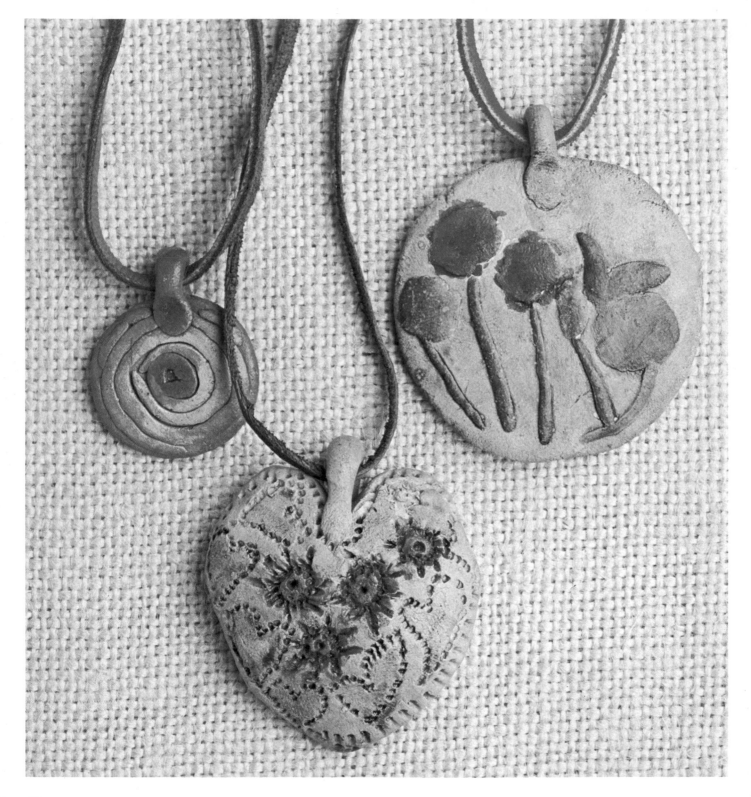

Clay beads

Clay is one of the most versatile materials for working jewelry – even the simplest techniques of pinching and modelling can produce exciting and original results – and now the widespread availability of self-hardening clay, ideal for small projects, means that you can work small pieces without using a kiln. You can start working in a basic way and, if your imagination is stimulated, then go on to working with natural clay and firing your designs.

Self-hardening clay

Self-hardening clay is a fairly new crafts material with exciting possibilities. It is like real clay and can be modelled and shaped in a variety of ways. Unlike natural clay, however, it can be left to dry out slowly until it becomes hard and durable. It is clean to use and, although it cannot be glazed, manufacturers supply varnishes which can be applied over painted decorations.

There are some varieties which can be oven-baked to lessen the hardening time (usually about 24 to 28 hours) but always check the instructions on the packet first to see if this is possible.

Natural clay

Natural clay has the great advantage of being an extremely cheap material. It does, however, require the use of a kiln to turn it into

Opposite: Pendants provide great scope for making individual patterns, whether they are a simple design, a name or a message. The pendants here show a coil, a heart with a design pricked on it and a round pendant with flower shapes.

Below: Working long beads from clay.
1. Roll lengths of clay between your hands.
2. To ensure a smooth and even finish, roll each coil with a flat piece of wood or a ceramic tile.

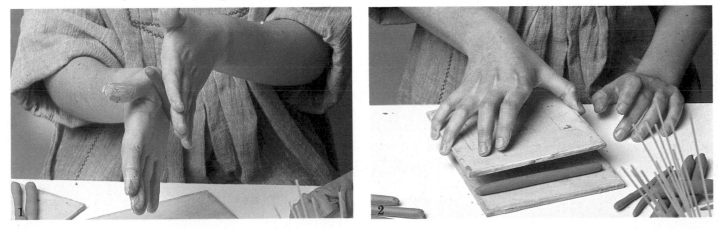

3. Using a knife, cut the coil into lengths.

4. To achieve an equal length, use the first bead as a guide.

5. Making the holes through the beads. Spaghetti is ideal as it will not stick to the clay.

6. Making round beads. Roll the cut lengths between the palms of your hands.

7. Impressing designs on the surface of the beads with a knife.

8. Painting the beads.

a hard, permanent material. Two types of clay are commercially available: white clay which is smooth, takes glaze well and is cleaner to use, and terracotta clay which fires to a pleasant red colour at a fairly low temperature.

Clay beads

Beads and other small projects are an ideal starting point for working in clay, giving you a good idea of the working properties of the material. Those shown below can be worked in either natural or self-hardening clay and can be decorated to give impressive finished results.

Working the beads

Long beads Roll lengths of clay between your hands (fig.1), then make them perfectly smooth and even by rolling each coil with a flat piece of wood or a ceramic tile (fig.2). Make several coils of the same thickness.

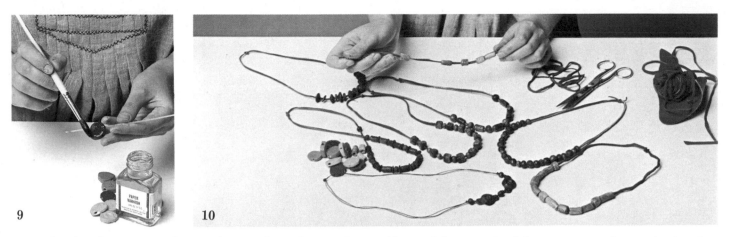

9

10

Use the knife to cut the coil into lengths – about 12mm-20mm ($\frac{1}{2}$in-$\frac{3}{4}$in) is a good length, although some could be smaller – rolling the coils as you do so (figs.3 and 4). This roll-and-slice movement prevents the coil being flattened.

Make holes with a thick piece of pointed wire, a needle, or even a piece of spaghetti which has the advantage of not sticking to the clay. Place the beads on newspaper to dry.

Round beads Roll out even coils of clay, this time making the coils thicker. To get balls the same size, cut equal lengths carefully. To make the balls, roll the cut lengths between the palms of your hands (figs.5 and 6). Make holes as before and leave to dry.

Square beads Roll a coil, then flatten it with a piece of wood if you want to make flat beads, or into a square block for square beads. Cut and pierce as before.

To finish

To finish the pieces, impress any designs at this stage (fig.7). When the clay is dry, smooth the surface with a damp sponge. Do not oversponge, as this will roughen the surface. If working with natural clay, fire to a temperature of about 980°-1000°C (1821°-1857°F).

If using self-hardening clay allow the pieces to dry for several days in the air, after which they will become very hard, although this clay can still be softened in water.

Thread the beads when they are completely dry on lengths of thin wire or spaghetti and paint them with poster paints or Indian [India] inks (fig.8). Leave to dry thoroughly and paint with a coat of clear varnish (fig.9).

Clay beads look attractive threaded on narrow suede strips (fig.10), which can be bought from hobby shops, or can be cut from suede scraps using scissors or a sharp blade.

9. *After painting, leave the beads to dry then paint with a coat of clear varnish.*

10. *Threading beads. Any cord strong enough will do but suede strips naturally complement the colour and texture of these clay beads.*

Clay necklace

You will need :
About 340gm ($\frac{3}{4}$lb) natural or self-hardening clay will make one necklace.
Tile or flat piece of wood.
Poster paints, Indian [India] inks or gouache colours.
Shapes for impressing.
Varnish.
Flat working surface, covered with hessian [burlap] or canvas for natural clay.
Smock or apron.
Suede strips about 3mm ($\frac{1}{10}$in) wide in suitable lengths for necklaces.

Clay is an extremely versatile material for working jewelry. Once the basic techniques have been mastered, all sorts of designs are possible, as intricate or as large as you like. These necklaces have been made in a variety of shapes and then painted in delicate pastel shades.

Badges and brooches

Making badges and brooches out of clay is slightly more difficult than the basic techniques used for making beads. However, by using simple modelling techniques anything from strikingly modern designs to more traditionally elegant pieces can be made.

To make the badges

First find your motif. For first projects it is better to stick to simple shapes such as squares and ovals as the more irregular shapes are likely to have a weak point.

Take as much modelling clay as you require and roll it out, using a

Below: An imaginative selection of clay badges and buttons. For first projects it is wise to stick to simple shapes but with a little practice lots of different designs can be worked.

Right: Inspiration for designs can be gleaned from many sources— a cartoon character, a picture in a magazine or even a favourite photograph can be all interpreted and made up into colourful brooches.
Opposite: A selection of farmyard brooches worked from a template. Details such as the legs should be marked on the damp clay with a needle to provide an outline for painting.

rolling pin or a clean bottle, to about 6mm ($\frac{1}{4}$in) thick. Don't make it thinner or it is likely to curl when drying or chip afterwards. Cut out the shape desired.

Smooth the surface with a wet finger or a damp cloth. Any additional details should be added at this point as they will adhere while drying and no glue will be needed.

If the clay begins to harden before you have finished modelling, simply moisten it with water. If you have to interrupt your work, it will remain malleable if you wrap a damp cloth around the clay or place it in a plastic bag.

Put the finished badge in a warm place to dry. Don't let it dry too quickly as it will then be very fragile and may warp. Turn several times during drying. The badge is completely dry when it goes lighter in tone and no longer feels soft. At this stage use an emery board to smooth away lumps and bumps around the edges. Do this very gently.

Now apply your colours. Poster paints are recommended as they give better cover and stronger colour. Paint the edges of the badge first, carrying the colour over to the back.

Cut a piece of felt to the shape of the badge. Trim slightly. Cut two slits in the felt opposite each other so that the back of a safety pin can be slotted into the felt. Cover the back of the badge with adhesive and put the felt and pin onto the badge.

When the glue has dried, hold the badge by the pin and apply water colour varnish to the painted surface. Protect the badge from dust until the varnish has dried. Apply a second coat when the first is completely dry.

The basic idea of making brooches from clay is almost endless in its variety. To achieve an unusual texture you may like to press tiny beads or silver balls (the kind used for decorating cakes) onto the

---

Clay badges

You will need:
Small quantity of self-hardening clay.
Rolling pin.
Water colours or poster paints.
Varnish.
Small pieces of felt.
Safety pins.
Emery boards and texture-making tools.
Strong adhesive.

surface of the clay while it is still soft. When the clay has hardened, paint around them carefully or directly over them as desired. For a glamorous effect, add a touch of glitter with a special gold or silver finish. This should be applied after first applying a coat of transparent varnish and allowing it to dry.

The farmyard brooches given below are yet another way of making more complex designs and again this can be developed by taking a favourite character in a children's cartoon strip and using this as a template, or even designing your own motif.

Farmyard brooches

Trace around each shape given opposite and transfer the outlines of the shapes to the card. Cut out each card to make a template. For each shape, take a small piece of clay and roll it out evenly until it is about 6mm ($\frac{1}{4}$in) thick. Place the card template on top of the clay and with the fine blade of a small knife cut out the shape.

You may prefer to prick out the shape with a needle, making a close dotted line. The small details on the sheep and the cow will have to be cut out this way as they are too small to cut out with a knife.

Once the shape has been cut out, smooth the rough edges with a wet finger. Mark any details, like the legs in the grass, with the blunt end of the needle.

Leave the pieces to dry. They must be kept flat and left to dry out thoroughly and slowly, it will be best if you can leave them overnight. Keep checking on the shapes every few hours to see that they do not warp. If the edges seem to be curling up, gently press them flat.

Details When you have cut out the basic sheep in clay, roll out tiny balls of clay between your finger and thumb. Roughen the surface of the sheep with your fingernails or the needle and gently moisten it. Press the tiny balls of clay onto the body until it is completely covered.

When the clay is completely dry it is ready to paint and varnish.

The mounts Try and get mounts that will cover a fairly large area on the back of each shape. The clay shapes are quite large and brittle so they will need the maximum amount of support from the mount. It would be a good idea to take a tracing of each brooch with you when you go to buy the mounts so you can choose the best mount for each one.

An epoxy resin consisting of two tubes of adhesive and a fixant, which have to be mixed together, is the best type of glue to use for attaching the shapes to the mounts. Follow the manufacturer's instructions for mixing the glue and the length of time needed for the glue to completely dry before wearing the brooches.

Farmyard brooches

You will need :
485gm (about 1$\frac{1}{4}$lb) self-hardening clay.
Poster paints or water colours.
Clear varnish.
Brooch mounts.
Quick-drying epoxy resin.
Tracing paper.
Thin card.
Scissors.
Small sharp knife.
Needle.

Trace patterns for the farmyard
brooches. Trace the patterns onto
a piece of stiff card and use as a
template for cutting the designs and
marking the detail.

Modelling flowers

Flowers make ideal subjects for clay jewelry. Their delicate and fragile structure can, with a little practice, be fashioned into delicate pieces to be fitted onto brooch mounts or on a smaller scale onto ear-ring or ring mounts. Make them to match fashion's romantic mood of the moment and to complement your prettiest clothes.

The rose brooch

Use your fingers to press out a strip of clay about 15cm (6in) long and 2cm ($\frac{3}{4}$in) wide. The edges should be slightly uneven, as this adds to the natural effect.

Begin rolling up the strip tightly at first to represent the centre of the flower, then more loosely to represent the outer petals. Continue rolling until the flower is complete, then pinch off the remainder of the strip.

Moisten the inner edge of the strip and press it firmly against the flower to secure it. Turn the rose over and, with a moistened fingertip, flatten the back to make a smooth surface.

Leave the rose to dry, then paint it. When the paint is dry, use an impact adhesive to secure the mount or finding in place on the back.

Rose brooch

You will need:
Lump of clay about the size of a ping-pong ball.
Poster paints and brush.
2.5cm (1in) brooch mount or finding.

Clay is ideal for modelling flower brooches, ear-rings or rings. These rose brooches are made by pressing out a strip of clay and then rolling it into a flower shape.

52

Flower brooches

Begin by taking a small piece of clay and rolling it into a small ball, approximately 1cm ($\frac{3}{8}$in) in diameter. Gently press the ball flat so that the edges do not crack. Press the clay more firmly at the outer edges than at the centre to achieve the delicate, wafer-thin appearance of flower petals. They are then quite easy to attach to the central petal.

The centre of the rose is made by rolling a petal into a tight curl, but enough clay should be left at the bottom with which to hold the rose while working. Each petal is pressed then pinched around the centre bud. Continue building up the rose in this way.

The leaves The leaves are made by pressing the clay out thinly then cutting them to shape with a craft knife or penknife. Take a pin and mark the edges of the leaves to give a crimped effect.

Finishing Cut the underside of the rose (the part you have been holding) off flush, so that the mounting pin will have a flat surface to adhere to. Put the rose aside to dry completely. When dry, paint the desired colour, mixing the paints to give a 'faded' effect.

Leave the paint to dry. When completely dry, coat the flower in varnish and glue the ear-ring or brooch mounting pin onto the back with an epoxy resin.

For a cluster of roses, make the roses smaller and press them into a round centre of clay.

For the basket of flowers, roll the clay out flat and cut out the basket shape. Make the wicker marks by pressing a pin into the clay. Make the tiny roses and leaves as before, then press them into the basket using a little water to moisten the clay if necessary. To finish, paint and varnish.

Flower brooches
You will need: 485gm (about 1¼lb) self-hardening clay. Brooch mounting pins and ear-ring mountings. Quick-drying epoxy resin. Poster paints. Varnish. Sable hair paint brush. Craft knife or penknife.

Left and above: A second method of working flowers is by shaping each petal separately. Clusters or baskets of flowers can also be worked this way and then fitted onto a brooch mount.

Wire jewelry

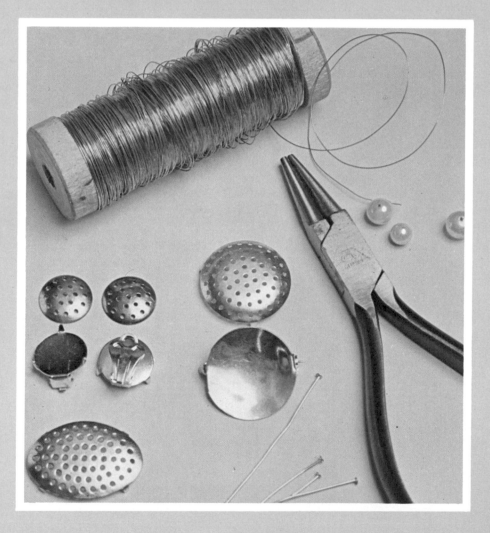

Brass wire jewelry

Brass wire is an excellent medium for starting to create designs with metal before going on to use the more expensive silver wire. You can experiment with any wire you can find as most are suitable for making jewelry. In any case, it's good practise and should something turn out particularly well, you can always copy it in silver.

Brass wire can be hard or soft. Either kind will do for making jewelry, but the soft wire will not retain its shape as well as the hard brass wire so, to counter this, you should use a slightly thicker diameter when working with soft wire.

Tools

Tools for working wire are very simple indeed, but it is wise to note that as you become more advanced in working with wire, the number of tools needed will increase and the techniques become more complex.

Round-nosed pliers These do not have to be expensive but check that the jaws make contact along their entire length. The inside of the jaws should be smooth otherwise they will damage the surface of the wire. If they are not smooth, cover the jaws with sticking plaster [bandaid], although this does make it slightly more difficult to grip heavy wire firmly. All-in-one pliers that cut and bend round and square lines are only suitable for simple projects.

Diagonal wire cutters or end cutters It is easier to cut jump rings (used in all aspects of jewelry) with the diagonal wire cutters, but either these or end cutters will do.

Metal file You can use a medium sized metal file or you can buy a selection of Swiss or needle files. You will not need all the files to make the pieces shown here, but it is economical to buy a set of about 6 as they will be useful if you intend to make more complicated articles.

Basic techniques

Jump rings These are used in all forms of jewelry for use in attaching and assembling pieces. To make two jump rings, place the end of the wire halfway down the jaws of the wire cutters.

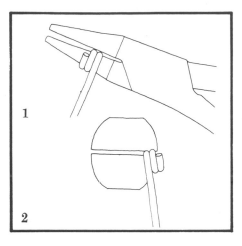

Work it around until you have two complete circles (fig.1). Line up the end of the cutters with the end of the wire and cut through both coils of wire (fig.2).

File the ends of the rings flat and smooth.

To make a larger number of jump rings, coil the wire around any cylindrical shape of the right size (fig.3).

Curling wire For this process you will need the round-nosed pliers. The size of the curl depends on the position of the wire in the jaws of the pliers. A small curl is made with the wire at the front of the pliers and a large one with it at the back. The end of the wire in the jaws should not stick out beyond the pliers. Grip the pliers firmly and turn in a clockwise direction using the thumb of the other hand to apply pressure to the wire, close to the jaws. You can work in a

Above: Jump rings are used in many forms of jewelry making to attach and assemble pieces. They can be bought, but it is easy to make them yourself.
1. Make two jump rings by placing the end of the wire halfway down the jaws of the wire or end cutters and work it around until you have two complete circles.
2. Line up the end cutters with the end of the wire and cut through both coils.
Right: This necklace is made up of jump rings of varying sizes. It can be made smaller by decreasing the number of jump rings.

The jump ring necklace

You will need:
42cm (17in) of 1.6mm (gauge 14-16) hard brass wire.
90cm (36in) of 1mm (gauge 18-19) hard brass wire.
Tools
Round nosed pliers, metal file. Diagonal wire cutters or end cutters.

counter-clockwise direction if you find it easier, but make it a habit to work in the same direction. Try to complete a curl without having to regrip the wire.

Hook and eye These are basically formed by the method of curling described above. However, they can sometimes be awkward so, if you have any left-over wire, practise making some first (fig.4).

Joins Note how joined pieces hang. The pieces do not stay flat but alternate – one flat and the other at right angles to it (fig.5). Designs must follow this pattern otherwise the piece of jewelry will not hang in the correct way. A piece of work will never appear the same when lying on the work bench as when it is suspended, so always hold your work up to look at it.

Polishing and finishing

Clean the completed pieces by immersing them in a liquid silver cleaner. Wash in soapy luke-warm water and dry. To prevent future discolouration, spray with a metal or clear varnish. If silver is being used with other materials, clean it thoroughly first.

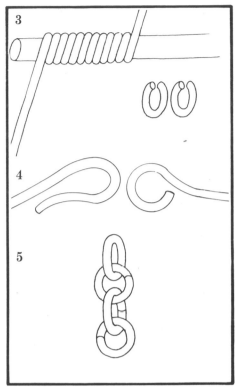

3. To make a larger number of jump rings, coil the wire around any shape of the right size.
4. The hook and eye for finishing the end of a neckband.
5. Joined rings should not stay flat but alternate.
Left: These ear-rings and the necklace are based on an abstract design starting in the centre with a circle then a triangle.

Necklace with ear-rings

You will need:
95cm (36in) of 1mm (gauge 18-19) hard brass wire.
42cm (17in) of 1.6mm (gauge 14-16) hard brass wire.
A pair of ear-ring findings with a hook and eye to which a jump ring can be attached.

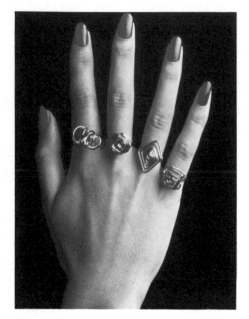

Above: These rings can be made with one or two coils of wire around the finger. If one coil is used the ends must be secured to prevent the ring from opening.

Below: Layered squares based on a curl.
Bottom: Series of loops at varying angles.

The jump ring necklace

This necklace is based on a series of jump rings assembled and attached to a neck band. You can vary the number and sizes of the jump rings to make a smaller or larger necklace.

The finished necklace is 37cm (15in) long. Use a piece of string to measure around your neck and add 5cm (2in) for the hook and eye at the back.

From the 1mm (gauge 18-19) wire, make 21 jump rings 1cm (⅜in) in diameter and 2 jump rings 2cm (⅞in) in diameter.

Cut off 7cm (2¾in) of the wire, file the ends and bend the wire into a 'V' shape. Make a hook at each end as shown in the illustration.

Make the neckband from the 1.6mm (gauge 14-16 wire) by shaping it with the fingers and making a hook and eye as in figure 4.

Assemble the jump rings as in the illustration and attach them to the neckband. Spray with metal varnish.

Necklace with ear-rings

The finished necklace measures 37cm (15in) long.

The neckband is made from the thicker gauge of wire. File the ends and make a hook and eye (fig.4).

The ear-rings are made from 26cm (10in) of thinner wire and based on an abstract design. Start the piece from the centre and finish by assembling with jump rings.

The pendant is made from 40cm (15in) of the thinner wire and assembled with a number of jump rings.

The rings

The rings can be made from 1mm (gauge 18-19) wire. You will need between 12cm (5in) and 25cm (10in) for a ring, depending on whether you take it around the finger once or twice and how intricate the design is. Always work from the inside of the design and finish by making the shank.

The chart below shows the approximate lengths of wire in different thicknesses. It will give some idea of length when you buy large quantities of copper, brass tinned copper or silver-plated wire.

Thickness =	Gauge		metres per kg	yards per lb
	B&S (USA)	SWG (UK)		
1.6mm =		14—16	56	28
1.5mm =		15—17	60	30
1 mm =		18—19	140	70
.8mm =		20—21	220	110
.6mm =		22 23	400	200

Wire and beads

Although many beads are worked on string a surprising amount of bead jewelry is made using metal pins or wire, and once the basic principles of wire jewelry are understood, necklaces, bracelets, earrings and brooches of apparently complicated natures become as easy to work as the simplest design. Furthermore, old jewelry can be re-styled or repaired and experiments with the permutations of colours and designs undertaken with confidence.

Essential materials

The gilt pins, fine silver wire and metal jewelry backings shown are the basic materials for this kind of beadwork. The pins are 5cm (2in) long and are used to attach beads to a chain or to make a linked chain of beads. The wire is used to attach beads to metal backings and any fine wire such as fuse wire or floral wire is suitable. Gilt pins and backings are available from some craft suppliers or bead specialist shops.

Applying beads to chains

The chunky necklace and bracelet in the photograph look elaborate but are really very simple to make and can be assembled from the kind of beads shown or from beads of your own choice.

The bracelet

Put a gilt pin through one of the largest beads and cut off all but 1.2cm (½in) of the protruding end (fig.1).
Bend the remaining end, using the pliers, into a loop to make a neat 'O'. When you do this try to bend the wire a little in the opposite direction from the way the loop is to go so the bead will hang properly and you will obtain a professional finish (see figs.2a and b). Repeat this with the three other large beads and space them along the chain so that the first one is about 2.5cm (1in) from the end of the chain. Now open the loops with the pliers, slip them onto the chain links and close them up again.
Do this with the 10 smallest beads, putting the first one on the second link from one end. It is important that all the beads are on

The bracelet

You will need :
19cm (7½in) of gilt chain with links about 6mm (¼in) long.
54 beads, including four 16mm (⅝in).
Ten 6mm (¼in) and 40 in-between sizes.
54 gilt pins.
Round-nosed pliers, wire cutters.
Bolt ring clasp.
Tape measure or ruler.

Below: Threading beads using wire.
1. Thread the bead onto a gilt pin and cut off the excess wire.
2. Bend the pin into a loop. Try to bend the wire a little in the opposite direction from the way the loop is to go so that the bead will hang correctly.

1   wrong   **2**   right

3. Cut the gilt pin to the size of the diameter of your bead plus 6mm ($\frac{1}{4}$in) extensions on each end. Make a round loop of the same size each end of the bead, open the loop slightly at one end and attach it to the loop of another bead.

4–6. Using metal backing plates.

4. Thread 14 beads onto the double wire, then secure them by twisting the two ends of wire together.

5. Taking the front half of the backing plate, convex side up, insert the wire into a hole on the outer edge.

6. Arrange the circle of beads on the plate so that the beads slightly overlap the plate edge.

the same side of the chain so that they hang properly when worn. When two or more beads are put on one link they can be attached to either the top or the bottom of the link.

Repeat the process with all the beads, putting one on each link, then filling in where colours look best. The beads should be fairly evenly spaced so there are no extra thick clusters anywhere.

Fix the bolt ring on the end loop and the bracelet is complete.

The necklace

The necklace is made in the same way as the bracelet but the beads are graduated to give more width and importance in the front.

Begin by placing one large bead in the centre of the chain.

Fix another large bead 2.5cm (1in) from it on either side.

Fix the other two large beads 4.5cm (1¾in) from the last two.

Now hang the smallest beads at equal intervals along the chain. This gives the basic framework of the necklace.

Divide the remaining beads into thirds and use one third for the 15cm (6in) at each end of the chain and the other two thirds for the remainder. This will build up the chunkiness in the front.

To complete, attach clasp.

Bead ropes

The glass and wooden bead necklace is made by a simple method that can be used to make ropes of beads of any length and combina-

The necklace

You will need :
40.5cm (16in) gilt chain with links about 6mm ($\frac{1}{4}$in) long.
110 beads, including 5 × 14mm ($\frac{5}{8}$in), twenty 6mm ($\frac{1}{4}$in),
16 × 4.5mm ($\frac{3}{16}$in) and 69 in-between sizes.
110 gilt pins.
Round-nosed pliers.
Bolt ring clasp.
Tape measure or ruler.

tion and which, unlike threaded beads, will not break in the course of normal wear if the links are properly closed.

These necklaces are made entirely with gilt pins and on long ropes which fit over your head, so clasps are not needed.

3

To make a rope remove the head from as many gilt pins as you require and at the same time cut the pin to the length you want. This is determined by the diameter of your bead plus 6mm ($\frac{1}{4}$in) extensions on both ends to make connecting links (fig.3). If beads of different sizes are used then divide the pins accordingly, for it is easier to cut several at a time.

Make a round loop of the same size at each end of each bead then, using your pliers to open the loop slightly at one end, attach it to the loop of another bead and continue until your rope reaches the desired length.

4

Using backing plates

Metal backing plates come in two parts; one part is covered in holes, the other has a plate to support the clasp and claws to hold the two pieces together. The two parts are joined by the claws after the beads are attached and this serves to cover up untidy wire ends and to make a functional finished object.

Backing plates are obtainable in various shapes and sizes and it is always necessary to plan your design so that the plate is completely covered in beads, which should extend slightly over the plate edge. Beads are attached with gilt pins or with wire which is threaded through the plate holes.

5

The brooch

Cut off 40.5cm (16in) of fine wire and fold it double so that you are using two thicknesses. Twist the loose ends together so that they will go through the holes in the beads.

Thread 14 beads onto this double wire so that they are roughly in the centre, then secure them by twisting the two ends of wire together to close the circle (fig.4). Do not trim.

Take the front half of the backing plate and, convex side up, insert the wire into a hole on outer edge (fig.5). Then arrange the bead circle on the plate so that the beads slightly overlap the plate edge (fig.6).

6

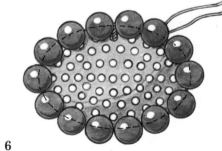

Holding beads and plate in one hand, count four holes; thread one wire up through the fourth hole in the outer edge, bring it over the bead circle and back down through the same hole (fig.7). Pull tightly and the wire will slip between two beads and help secure the circle to the plate.

Repeat this at equal intervals around the circle, then twist the

7

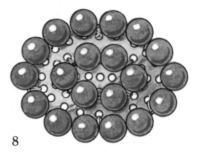

8

remaining wire together and cut off surplus.

To make inner circle use 6 beads and a 25cm (10in) piece of wire folded double. Proceed to make an inner circle (fig.8) in the same manner as before except this time secure the beads to the plate by threading wire in between every other bead, instead of every fourth one.

7. Securing the beads onto the plate using wire.
8. Positioning the inner circle of beads.

Right: A lovely combination of beads make up this elegant bead rope. The links are made from gilt pins and so are less likely to break.

The brooch

You will need:
Roll of fine wire such as fuse wire or floral binding wire.
Round-nosed pliers.
Three gilt pins.
Oval backing plate 3cm (1¼in) long.
Thirty-eight 5mm ($\frac{3}{16}$in) beads.

The third circle has 12 beads strung on 50cm (20in) of doubled wire. Place it in the gap between the other two circles (it will protrude somewhat) and push the wire through a hole below. It is rather more difficult to attach this circle and you must take care not to pull too tightly as you hook the wire between the beads or they will sit unevenly. It doesn't matter if the wire does not go back through the same hole as long as it goes through the next one (as the plate gets crowded with beads it becomes more difficult to be accurate).

The centre can be made with just one round bead mounted with a gilt pin or with two drop lengths as shown.

To mount one bead using a gilt pin, secure it to the backing with a loop as in fig.2, then flatten the loop against the backing.

To make drop lengths the pin must go in the reverse way and the loop be made in front of the bead. This way other beads can be added by linking (fig.9).

The drops shown are of uneven lengths. Attach beads with two links (fig.3) and add two beads to one chain and three to the other. This completes the drop lengths.

Fix the brooch to the other half of the plate by putting the two parts together and pressing the claws down firmly with the pliers.

The matching ear-rings are made in exactly the same way but with one circle of 6 beads plus a centre bead. Use a smaller backing plate, 5mm ($\frac{3}{16}$in) in diameter. The beads are threaded onto a 30cm (12in) length of wire bent double.

9

To make drop lengths the pin must go in the reverse way so that the other bead can be added by linking.

Below: Brooch and ear-rings made using a metal backing plates. Below left: Beads are attached to backing plates with wire or gilt pins which are threaded through the holes of the plate.

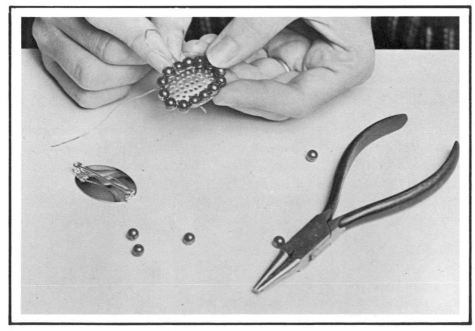

Wire and clay

Left: A simple yet effective choker using clay beads threaded on wire.
1. Having cut the wire to the length required, bend one end over to form a loop.
2. Having threaded the beads, bend the other end over in the same way.
3. Positioning the knitting needle in the drill (top view).

These attractive and original necklaces are made from oven-baked clay beads, painted with bright enamel paint and threaded or linked with jeweler's wire. The beads can be left plain, interspersed with bought beads for contrast, or made in a variety of shapes and sizes to create individual and unusual jewelry.

The red choker

Make 26 clay beads (see Jewelry from Clay), grading the sizes from large beads, to position at the centre front, through successively smaller pairs, so that the beads at the centre back of the choker are approximately half the size of the front ones. Leave the beads to dry overnight. Bake the beads in the oven to harden them finally, following the instruction on the pack.

When the beads are cool, they are ready to paint. A useful paint rack can be made by rolling out a long sausage of clay and sticking a row of toothpicks vertically into it. First paint the top half of the bead, then turn it upside down, place on the paint rack and paint the underside. The beads illustrated here are painted with bright red enamel paint.

Measure the circumference of the neck and cut off a length of 16 gauge wire equal to this length. Bend the wire gently so that it curves around the neck. Using the round pliers, bend one end of the wire over to form a ring (fig.1).

Lay the painted beads out in the size sequence and begin threading them onto the wire. The necklace illustrated here has small black glass beads positioned between the red beads, and the necklace is finished off at each end with two black beads. Use the round pliers to bend the other end of the wire carefully over to form a loop as shown in fig.2.

The links

Take a hand drill and clamp it in a bench vice in such a way that the drill may be freely rotated. Take the No.9 [U.S. size 4] knitting needle and place the pointed end in the drill (fig.3). Take a length of 18 gauge wire and make a right-angled bend at one end. Hook this short end into any one of the spaces between the three jaws of the chuck (fig.4). The wire should pass over the front of the needle. Now grip the knitting needle with the right hand as if it were a pencil, placing the thumb on the section of wire which passes over the knitting needle. With the left hand, slowly turn the handle of the drill so that the knitting needle revolves in the direction indicated in fig.4. This will make the wire wind up on the needle to form a coil. Guide the wire with the thumb as it is winding so that

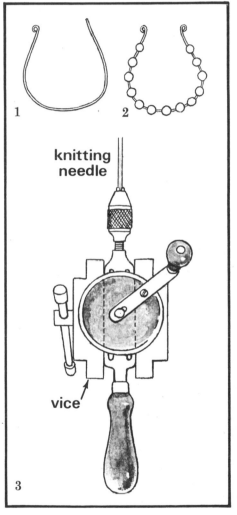

1

2

knitting
needle

vice

3

Right: The green and white necklace. Using a small white bead at the centre, the beads are then linked together using jeweler's wire.

the coil is very tight. When all the wire is wound around the needle, the coil can be pulled off.

To cut the links from the coil, take the coil in the left hand and hold it vertically between the thumb and first finger, press the coil against a table top. Use the jewelry piercing saw to cut through the top of the coil (fig.5).

As the blade cuts through the top of the coil, the first link falls away. Always hold the coil tightly between the thumb and first finger while sawing. Do not use too thick a blade to cut the links or the gap in the link will be too large to close securely. Always use two pairs of flat pliers to open the links (fig.6) and to pinch them closed.

Make two chains each composed of eight links. Link the chains to the ends of the choker as shown (fig.7).

Make two hooks (fig.8) and link to the chains to complete the necklace.

Green and white beads

Make 11 pairs of green beads, graded in size, by rolling out a 'sausage' of clay, thicker at one end and tapering towards the other

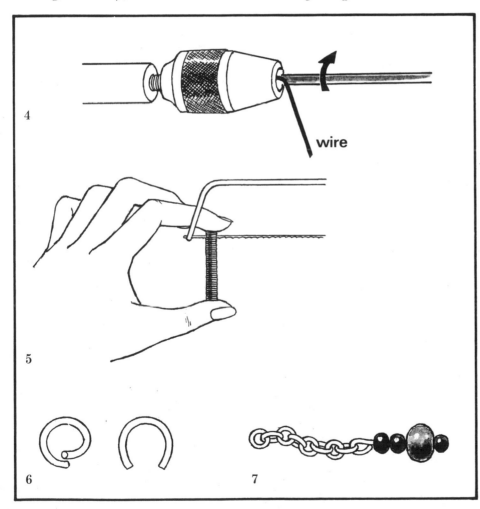

4. Placing the wire in the drill.
5. Cutting the links from the coil.
6. Opening the links, incorrectly and correctly.
7. The chains linked to the choker.

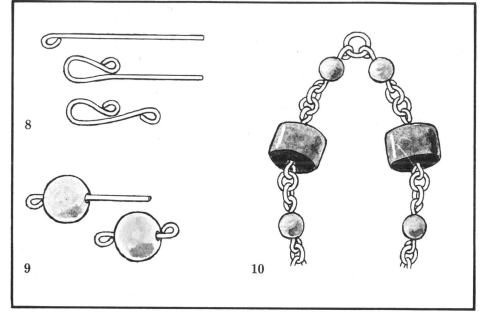

end. Slice off the beads with a sharp knife and make the centre holes with a toothpick. Make 23 small round beads as described above, and bake the beads in the same way. Paint the large tubular beads bright green with enamel paint. The smaller beads are left plain.

Wire each bead up as follows. Pass one end of a length of wire through the bead, and use the round pliers to bend the end over to form a loop (fig.9).

Cut the wire, leaving a length sufficient to make a loop on the other side of the bead.

Make a number of links as described for the red choker (above), and pass a link through the loop at each side of each bead. Begin the necklace at the centre front with a small white bead, and use a third link at each side to join both sides of the centre bead to the largest of the pairs of green beads. Continue linking the beads in this way until ten green beads and eleven white beads are linked ending with a white bead at each end. Join the two white beads with a slightly larger link, made on No.7 [U.S. No.6] knitting needle (fig.10). Link two more white beads into the larger link, and continue threading the beads until there are 12 white and 12 green beads in the upper part of the necklace, ending with a green bead at each end. From the last bead link two small links and one large link.

Make a hook using the method described above to complete the necklace.

Wire wrapping techniques

Wire wrapping is a jewelry technique which is mainly used for displaying polished or unpolished stones and is another way that wire can be used in conjunction with other materials not only as a means of linking them together but in fact to enhance the appearance of the finished pieces.

To link the stones use wire that will hold them securely, i.e. the larger the stone, the thicker the wire should be. You can use any wire but try to find some that shows off the stones at their best. Rough stones do not need very fine wire but smaller, smoother stones look better in silver wire. You can use brass, copper, silver, silver-plated or even fuse wire.

To make the necklace

The method described here for making the necklace can also be used for a bracelet or ear-rings. The ear-rings will need findings from a jeweler to complete the assembly.

For an average-sized necklace the completed length should be about 56cm (22in).

To wrap the stones you will need about 15cm (6in) of wire to wrap around each stone, depending on its size. The wire should be longer rather than shorter as you can always cut off excess but if it is too short the entire piece of wire will be wasted.

Arrange the stones in the sequence you want to use them, leaving a gap of 2cm ($\frac{3}{4}$in) between each one.

Using the round-nosed pliers make a loop at one end of the wire to hold the jump ring.

Hold this to the stone in the position you want it. Bend the length of wire around the stone, working from the looped end and holding it tightly in position. Work towards the other end of the stone, bending the wire to follow the curves of the stone.

Make sure that there are no sharp pieces of wire sticking out as they will catch on clothing or scratch the skin.

Make the jump rings and assemble the stones. Depending on the necklace length you require, use a jump ring between each stone, or three for a longer length, but always use an odd number, otherwise

Above: Necklace and ear-rings made with pebbles and wrapped using silver-plated wire.

The necklace
You will need: Jump rings, 1cm ($\frac{3}{8}$in) diameter, about 19. A selection of stones or pebbles. 1.5mm (gauge 15) silver-plated wire. **Tools** Round-nosed pliers. Side or diagonal wire cutters. Metal file.

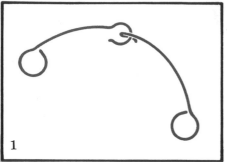

1

1. *Shaping the ends of the wire.*
2, 3. *Bending the wire before wrapping.*
4. *Twisting the two pieces of wire together.*
5. *Bending the loop down to make a hook.*
6. *Making the cage for the tumbled stones.*

Right: Bracelet and ear-rings made with tumbled amethysts.

the stone will not hang as planned. Make sure the front of the stone will face the correct way when assembled.

To make the ends, measure the length of the arranged stones and subtract this length from the length of the completed necklace. This will give you the length required for the two ends. For example if it is 16cm (6in), then 8cm (3in) must be the length of each completed end. Add 4cm (1$\frac{1}{2}$in) to the end length and cut the wire. File any sharp ends.

Make a large loop at one end of each piece using the round-nosed pliers. These will be attached to jump rings to assemble the necklace. At the other end make a U-shaped bend and turn the ends slightly away from the longer length. Shape the entire length so that the two pieces will hook into each other (fig.1).

Bracelet and ear-rings

Very little equipment is needed for this simple bracelet. You can use any tumbled stones you like but choose ones that are roughly the same size and shape, with blending colours.

Measure the wrist with a tape measure and to this length add 5cm (2in) to allow for the bulk of the stones and for comfort. If this measurement is over 19cm (7½in) you will probably need 6 stones, if less, only 5. If there is any doubt lay the stones in a row, allowing 2cm (¾in) between each one and 6mm (¼in) to spare at each end. For each stone cut 2 pieces of silver wire both 10cm (4in) long. Bend one piece in the middle (fig.2).

Hold the straight ends in the fingers and the loop with the pliers. Twist around in a full circle to make the loop secure. Repeat with the other pieces of wire (fig.3).

Lay two pieces side by side with the loops at opposite ends and take one straight end and twist it around the base of the loop nearest it (fig.4). Do the same with the other end. Take care that the wire lies flat and makes a neat twist. Snip off the end after 2 complete turns and press in the end. Do the same to the other ends, thus making a wire cage with a loop at each end. The wires of the cage should be pulled out to form an oval shape so that the tumbled stone will slip inside easily, allowing a small space at both ends.

Holding the stone inside the cage, grip the wire with the pliers and make a zig-zag shape that lies flat on the stone. This will take a little thought and practice so study the stone carefully so you can show off its shape to advantage.

This bending shortens the wires so that the twisted loops sit snugly at each end of the stone. A gentle half twist of the pliers will tighten them further. Repeat all this with each of the stones for the bracelet. To join the stones together, open a jump ring just enough to slide the loop of two stones through it, then press together firmly. Repeat with all the others.

Attach the bolt ring clasp to one end to complete the bracelet. As an alternative to the bolt ring clasp you can make a hook from a piece of wire. Double 4cm (1½in) of wire and press the fold as close together as possible. Cut the straight ends even. Using the pliers turn these ends into a loop which goes through the loop at the end of a stone. Bend the loop down to make a hook (fig.5). The ear-rings are made on the same principle as the bracelet, but the cages are made with a loop at one end only.

Take 2 pieces of wire 9cm (3½in) long and twist them together with 3 turns in the middle.

Bend all 4 ends upwards and with one end make a loop with the pliers, twisting the wire back on itself to secure. The end of this loop is laid down on the wire and the other ends twisted neatly around it 3 times and then cut off and pressed down (fig.6).

This makes the cage for the tumbled stone, so proceed to secure the stone as before. This time make sure that the twist at the bottom does not get pulled to one side when the wires are bent into shape. Connect the loops to the findings to complete the ear-rings.

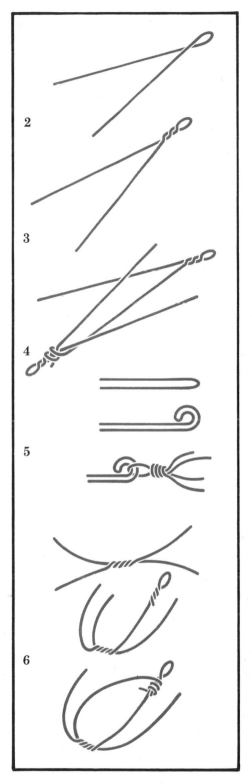

2

3

4

5

6

Twisted silver wire jewelry

Twisting silver wire provides a number of textures which can be used in many ways to make jewelry and ornaments. The bracelet and rings, shown here, were made from round silver wire, but you may wish to experiment with the many different shapes and sizes of wire available.

Twisted wire bracelet

You will need :
78cm (30in) of 1.6mm (gauge 14-16) round silver wire.
A jeweler's piercing saw and pencil.
Hand drill and clamp or bench vice.
Asbestos mat, borax flux, alum pickle, jewelers' rouge, detergent and a soft cloth.
Medium silver solder.
Blowtorch, file and pair of pliers.

Twisting wire

This technique involves twisting two or more strands of silver wire to form a patterned length of silver. In order to get a consistent and tight twist, a hand drill is used. The wires to be twisted are fastened into the jaws of the drill. The other ends of the wires are then attached to a clamp and kept taut while the crank of the drill is turned, thus twisting the wire. Any wire can be twisted in this way though some of the stronger steel wire might prove more difficult.

Bracelet

The bracelet is very simple to make. It has no fastening clasp as it is made just big enough to slide over your hand. Twisted silver wire of the same texture can be used equally well in other jewelry designs.

Wind the length of silver wire around and around your hand to form a rough circle about 7.5cm (3in) in diameter and tuck in the ends so that the wire will not uncoil.

Place on the asbestos mat and anneal with the blowtorch.

To do this, heat the wire all over taking care to move the flame steadily around the circle of wire as too much heat in one place might melt or distort the metal. When the wire is a dull red colour, remove the flame and cool the wire in water.

When the wire is cool, unwind it and put one end in the vice or clamp. Holding the other end with the pliers, pull the wire as taut as possible and as straight as you can get it. The wire should be quite soft after annealing and should feel as though it is stretching slightly when you pull it straight.

Fold the wire carefully in half and place the folded end in the clamp or vice. The other ends are placed firmly in the drill jaws making sure that both ends are secure and the wires straight and even (fig.1).

Hold the drill in your hand, keeping the wire between the drill and clamp taut. Then, slowly, begin to turn the crank handle of the drill, still keeping the wire taut. This serves to twist the two wires together—the more you turn the drill the tighter the twist. Rely on your judgement to decide how tight you want the twist, but for the best proportions with this thickness of wire, there should be at least three twists every 2.5cm (1in). In the bracelet illustrated here, there are three and a half twists to every 2.5cm (1in).

Remove the wire from the drill and clamp and cut off the folded end. The twisting process hardens the wire so it must be annealed again to soften it.

When the twisted wire has cooled, bend it gently in your fingers to form a circle just big enough to slide over your hand. This initial

Below: Some of the fascinating effects that can be achieved by twisting silver wire. In these pieces round silver wire is used but you can experiment with other shapes or types of wire.

fitting is important because if it is too large it will slide off too easily when finished and if too small, you will not be able to get it on.

Mark the size with a pencil and, using the jeweler's piercing saw, cut off the piece for the bracelet. Keep the remaining twisted wire to make the ring.

File the ends of the bracelet flat to ensure a join good and butt them together as closely as possible.

The two ends will be joined together by soldering so try to arrange the wire so that the twist will look continuous. This might entail cutting or filing off a minute piece of the wire.

Place the bracelet on the asbestos mat and flux the join with borax. Flux is a chemical compound that prepares the metal surfaces for joining by helping the molten solder to flow smoothly and dissolves the oxides that form on the metal during heating. It should only be applied on the part of the metal where solder is required and the metal around the joint must be cleaned with a file or an abrasive paper.

Soldering

Silver soldering is a technique used on small items such as jewelry and provides a strong joint. Place a very small piece of solder along the join and heat with a blowtorch until it is a dull red. Remove the flame immediately the solder begins to flow and join the two ends. Place the bracelet in an alum pickle, then wash in soap and water and dry.

To get the bracelet to a perfect circle, you must push it onto a suitable shape. In this case the wire was pushed down firmly over the neck of a bottle of a suitable size until it was even and circular. Try the bracelet for size. If you were careful with the initial fitting, it should be perfect. However, if it should happen to be too large, you can cut a piece out and re-solder the ends together. If this is not necessary, you can go ahead with the polishing.

As there has been very little filing, there should not be any scratches on the wire. It will therefore only need to be rubbed firmly with jeweler's rouge on a soft cloth, washed in detergent and polished again with a clean, dry cloth. It is now ready to wear.

Rings

A ring can be made from the remainder of the twisted wire used for the bracelet. You will need the same tools and materials as for the bracelet but, in addition, you will need a leather or wooden mallet and a ring stick.

Hammer the piece of twisted wire on the ring stick to form a circle. Start from either end and work towards the middle of the wire.

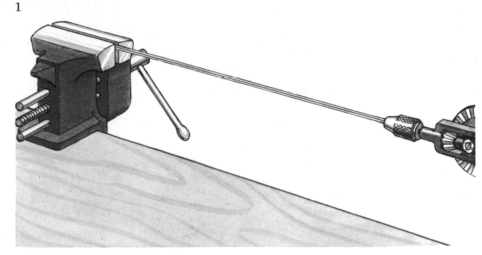

1

1. To start twisting the wire, fasten the wire into the drill jaws and the vice. Keep the wire taut while turning the crank handle to twist it.

When you have fashioned the wire into a circle, try it for size on the finger on which you intend wearing it. Cut to the required size and solder the same way as the bracelet.

Make the ring into a perfect circle by hammering it on the ring stick. Be careful not to hammer too hard as this may flatten the twists and spoil the shape.

Clean and polish as for the bracelet.

Flattened wire ring

Another interesting use of this twist method is to use wires of different thicknesses and then hammer the twisted strands flat before making the ring. The ring can then be as small and thin as you choose.

This ring is made from three wires, two thin and one slightly thicker.

Wrap the 40cm (16in) of 0.7mm (gauge 21-22) silver wire around and around your hand and fold in the ends so that the wire will not uncoil.

Place the wire on the asbestos mat and anneal (see above).

When it is cool, fasten one end in the clamp or vice and pull straight.

Fold the wire carefully in half, putting the two ends in the drill jaws and the folded end in the clamp. Twist as for the bracelet. You should be left with a 12.5cm (5in) length of twisted wire.

Take the length of 1mm (gauge 18-19) silver wire and put one end of this and one end of the twisted wire into the vice or clamp and the other ends in the drill jaw.

Make sure that the two sections of wire are pulled as straight as possible and then twist them together.

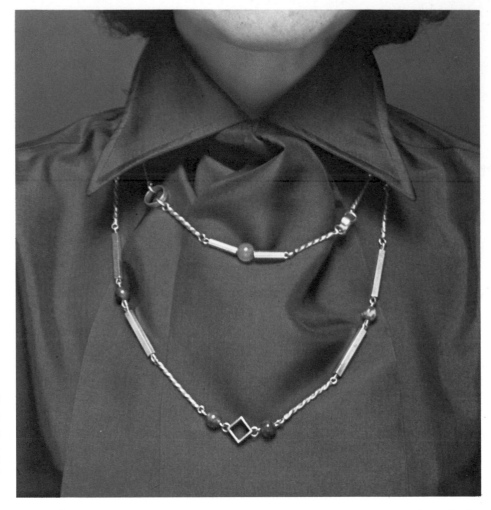

Right: Interesting effects can be achieved by mixing different textures of wire. These necklaces are worked by using twisted wire with silver tubing and beads.

Note: be sure that the twists are evenly distributed along the whole length of the wire.

Remove the twisted wire from the vice and drill, place on the asbestos mat and anneal to soften.

When the twisted wire has cooled, lay it flat on the steel block. With the planishing hammer, flatten the wire along the whole length. Do not hit too hard at any point but make sure the wire is an even thickness. Repeat the annealing as hammering hardens the metal.

Bend the flattened twisted wire around to fit the finger on which it is to be worn and mark with a pencil. With the piercing saw, cut off the excess wire and file the ends flat.

Use a mallet and ring stick to shape the ring. Join with medium solder, making sure that the pattern of the twists meet up so the join will not be obvious.

This ring will need more polishing than the other one as it has been hammered. Start with fine emery paper, then use tripoli on a soft cloth and finish with jeweler's rouge. The result should be a beautifully polished, textured ring.

Fine wire rings

Wire of almost any shape can be twisted together to produce an unusual effect. A small silver ring can be made from fine wire which is loosely twisted, so that when it is hammered, the twists will part slightly to give the ring a lacy appearance.

Necklaces

Another use for twisted wire is to make it into links for a necklace. An interesting range of permutations for these can be achieved, as the examples indicate. The necklaces make use of beads which can be bought, or made from clay, and links from silver tubing. This tubing comes in a variety of shapes and sizes. It is usually bought in 2.5cm (1in) lengths and is sawn easily into slices.

The necklace with the green beads uses two sizes of square tubing and is excellent practice for soldering very small links. The twist links are made of two different thicknesses of wire. The necklace is 57cm (22½in) long.

First take 35cm (14in) of both the 0.7mm (gauge 21-22) and 1.6m (gauge 14-16) silver wire, anneal and straighten.

Using the drill and clamp, twist the two pieces of wire together. Keep a lot of pressure on the wire to make sure that the thick wire bends around the thin one to the same degree as the thin does around the thick.

Saw the twisted wire into six even pieces about 3m (1⅛in) long. Straighten the pieces with your fingers and file the ends flat.

Now cut the tube. Make sure that one end is square by filing it flat. Begin with the larger piece of tubing.

Take a pair of dividers and spread the points 2.5cm (1in) apart. With one point touching the flat end of the tube, scratch a line 2.5cm (1in) up the tube with the other point. Make sure the line goes all the way around the tube.

Continue marking off 2.5cm (1in) sections on the tube until it is divided into six sections.

With the piercing saw, carefully cut off the sections, making sure that the saw is not going crooked by checking with the lines on the sides of the tube.

Set the pair of dividers at 4mm ($\frac{3}{16}$in) and mark off these lengths on the short, thicker piece of tubing.

Cut off these sections. You may find that you have to hold the

The necklace
You will need: 100cm (40in) of 0.7mm (gauge 21-22) round silver wire. 35cm (14in) of 1.6mm (gauge 14-16) round silver wire. 1.2cm ($\frac{9}{16}$in) of silver tube, 10mm ($\frac{3}{8}$in) square. 15cm (6in) of silver tube, 3mm ($\frac{1}{8}$in) square. Nine glass or ceramic beads about 6mm ($\frac{1}{4}$in) in diameter. Pair of dividers, some thin strips of asbestos and tripoli. Dowel, or steel knitting needle, 3mm ($\frac{1}{8}$in) thick. Other tools and materials as for the bracelet.

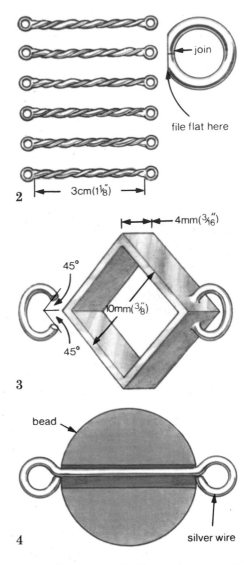

tubing in a pair of pliers to get a proper grip when sawing.

You will now need to make 18 small jump rings, about 3mm ($\frac{1}{8}$in) in diameter. These are made by annealing 11.5cm ($4\frac{1}{2}$in) of the 0.7mm (gauge 21-22) wire and then winding it around a dowel or knitting needle.

Slide the coil of wire to the end of dowel and cut through one side of the wire, pushing the wire to the end of the dowel as each link is separated. One of these jump rings must be soldered to each end of the twisted wire links.

Take 12 jump rings, make sure they are quite round and file the ends so that they join as closely as possible.

File the wire flat at the join so that it is half its original thickness (fig.2). Do this to all 12 jump rings.

Put all the twisted wire links and prepared jump rings on the asbestos mat. The flattened side of the jump rings must be pressed close to the flat ends of the twisted pieces (see fig.2).

Borax all the places to be joined and put a small piece of medium solder on each join. Heat until solder runs, allow to cool and then pickle. You will be left with six twisted wire links with jump rings soldered on each end (see fig.2).

The remaining jump rings must be soldered to the large square links. First open up the jump rings and file the ends to an angle of 45°, to ensure they will sit snugly on the corners of the link (fig.3).

When soldering the jump rings into position on the 10mm ($\frac{3}{8}$in) square silver tubing, the jump rings will have to be raised a little to be half way up the thickness of the tube. To do this, place a thin piece of asbestos underneath the jump rings so that they are at the right height for soldering.

The beads and the small square tubing are then strung on the rest of the 0.7mm (gauge 21-22) wire. Loops are made at each end and turned over with pliers so that the loose end can be tucked back against the bead (fig.4). Do not solder these as the heat would crack the bead and melt the thin tubing. Polish all parts of the necklace separately with tripoli, then jeweler's rouge on a soft cloth. As there should not be any scratches on the silver this polishing should be sufficient.

Now join all the pieces together. Open the unsoldered links, i.e. those through the beads and small square tubing, and thread the fixed jump rings onto them. The sequence is bead, thin square tubing, twisted wire link, bead, large square link, bead, twisted wire link, thin square tubing and then back to the bead and repeat the procedure.

A final polish with a soft cloth and the necklace is finished. There is no fastening as it should be large enough to slip over your head.

2. Detail of filed jump ring and twisted silver wire cut to length.
3. File the jump rings to fit the corner of the square link.
4. Bend the wire to form a fastening on each side of the beads.

Using
natural materials

Pebble polishing techniques

Jewelry from polished or even unpolished rocks and pebbles is probably the oldest and most fascinating of all the crafts – and your involvement can be as simple or as extensive as you like, and almost as cheap or as costly as you decide.

You can go out and collect stones yourself or buy them at a shop; you can polish pebbles until they have a permanent shine, or you can buy them ready polished. You can make up polished stones into jewelry, using your own base or bought settings which can be cheap gilt ones or expensive settings in silver or gold. The joy of the craft comes from the beauty of the stones themselves – and the part you can play in bringing this out.

Right: Carefully matched tumbled jasper pebbles make up this elegant necklace. The stones are attached to the necklace chain by means of the bell cap finding.

Gemstone jewelry
You will need :
Polished stones.
Findings.
Epoxy resin adhesive.
Saucer for mixing adhesive.
Match-sticks for applying adhesive.
Jewelry pliers or tweezers.
Spirit [turpentine].
Clean rags.
Shallow tray or tin.
Salt or sand.

Equipment

The best way of polishing pebbles is to use a tumbling machine. These are not expensive and can be purchased from a good crafts shop. For the beginner, however, there are tumbling kits which include all the necessary equipment for polishing the pebbles you have already collected. Apart from the tumbling machine, they include the necessary grits and polishing agents, epoxy resin glue, a selection of findings or jewelry mounts to which you attach your polished stones and even a batch of stones for polishing.

Polishing pebbles

A tumbling machine consists of a small barrel and two parallel rollers. These are turned by pulleys, and a rubber belt, driven by an electric motor.

First, place the pebbles in the barrel and fill it with water. Add one tablespoon of coarse silicon carbide grit (80 grade) to the water and secure the lid firmly to the barrel, which is then placed onto the rollers. The barrel is then turned on the rollers, at a speed of approximately one revolution per second, for the next seven days. While this process is going on the pebbles will roll, or 'tumble', against each other as the barrel turns, and the silicon carbide grit will gradually wear away all surface roughness.

When the first stage is completed, remove the barrel from the rollers and wash the pebbles thoroughly in fresh water to remove all traces of the coarse silicon carbide.

The barrel will contain quite a lot of sludge at this stage. Do not pour this down the sink or you will run the risk of blocking the plumbing. Simply empty into a plastic bag and throw it away.

Rinse the barrel thoroughly to make sure that all traces of grit have been removed. Put the pebbles back into the barrel and fill up with clean water once more. Having done this, add one tablespoonful of medium silicon carbite grit (220 grade) to the water, and repeat the tumbling process for a further seven days. During this second stage, surface scratches caused by the coarse silicon carbide are removed from the pebbles. At the end of the second seven day period you should remove the pebbles from the barrel and wash them carefully under running water. You should now clean the barrel thoroughly once more. Now, the entire process should be repeated for a third time – this time using fine silicon carbide (440 grade). This will give a smooth matt finish to each pebble.

After three weeks of continuous rotation inside the barrel, the pebbles should be absolutely smooth and ready to take their final polish. However, you must first remove all traces of silicon carbide on the pebbles and from the inside of the barrel or you will fail to

Right: A tumbling machine, together with a second barrel, This machine is constructed so that the second barrel, which is sold separately, runs from the same motor as the first and can be geared to run at high speed for rough tumbling or at low speed for polishing.

achieve a high polish during the final stage. Place the pebbles back in the barrel, fill it up with clean water and add one teaspoonful of tin oxide or cerium oxide. Allow the pebbles to tumble inside the barrel for approximately twenty four hours. After this has been done, the pebbles will be polished to a brilliance which will enhance their natural colours and beauty. You should now give the pebbles a final rinse under running water.

Rules for polishing

The two main points to remember for successful polishing are:

1. Always load the barrel with pebbles of a similar hardness. It is easy to carry out a 'hardness test' when collecting your pebbles. Take a small penknife with you when searching a beach for likely specimens. As you pick up each pebble, scratch its surface with the blade of the knife. Put all those which cannot be scratched by the knife into one bag, and those which are easily scratched into another.

2. Include as wide a variety of pebble sizes as possible when filling the barrel. You should never load your machine with pebbles of a uniform size.

Findings for tumbled stones

This chapter illustrates a representative cross-section of the findings to be found in lapidary and craft shops, and gives advice on deciding which findings are best suited to various sorts of stones.

Most shops sell findings for ear-rings, brooches, bracelets, necklaces, pendants, rings, tie clips and pins – almost any jewelry you may want to make – in a variety of designs, sizes and different metals suitable for baroque (irregularly shaped) tumbled and polished stones.

Findings can be small and fine to complement delicate-looking small stones, or big and sturdy for large heavy stones. Styles vary from simple to ornate, and traditional to modern. Simple styles are easier to work on so it's wise to avoid ornate or filigree designs for your first attempt.

There is usually a choice of metals too – and prices vary accordingly. Some metal findings are very cheap indeed and, however attractive your stones, are liable to make the finished articles of jewelry look cheap. Well made, handsome findings in base metals cost a little more but are worth paying for because they can transform the same tumbled stones into really elegant looking pieces of jewelry. Brass and steel can be strong, and usually have a gilt or silver coloured finish. Stainless steel is also available for some types of findings, and you can choose either a brushed or polished finish. Sterling silver and 9ct. gold findings are considerably more expensive. It's no more difficult to set stones in these metals but it's obviously a good idea for the beginner to try her hand at jewelry making with the cheaper base metals first. Moreover, silver and gold findings are usually specially designed to take the more expensive faceted stones and cabochons, and it may be difficult to find one which provides a suitably comfortable fit for a baroque tumbled stone.

The three basic findings

Whatever article of jewelry you are making, whether it be a pair of ear-rings or a bracelet, your stone will be bonded to one of three basic types of finding – bell cap, pad mount, or claw setting. The

1. *Bell caps can be plain or ornate and come in many different sizes.*
2a. *Another form of bell cap, the leaf bail, has only two prongs and is used for suspending a flat stone.*
2b. *Jump rings are used in many forms of jewelry and can be made or bought in a variety of sizes.*

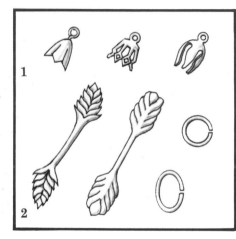

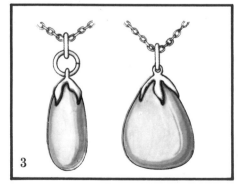

3. *The bell cap eyelet and the best facet of the stone should face you during bonding. To keep the best facet facing outwards, use one jump ring only to connect bell cap to chain or use any other odd number to give extra length.*
Right: A beautifully marked stone attached by means of a suitably ornate bell cap finding.

84

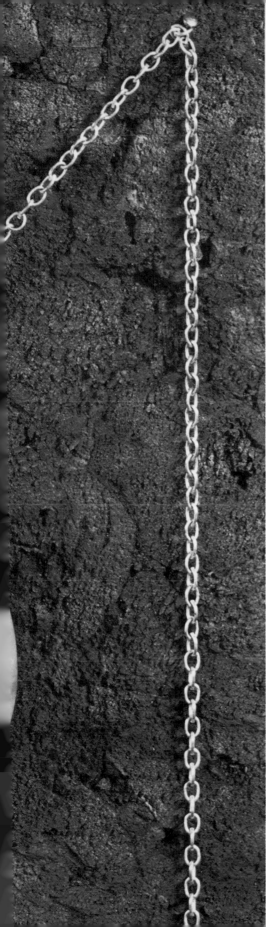

most fundamental factor in selecting the right finding lies in deciding which of these basic types is most suited to your stones – a decision which should be determined by the shape of the stone itself.

Bell caps

The majority of bell caps (fig.1) are very like their name, being bell-shaped in appearance. They have either four or seven prongs and provide the means for suspending a stone. They are frequently used for pendants, drop ear-rings and for attaching hanging stones to bracelets. Pear shaped, oblong or 'drop' stones that taper to a point are most suitable for these bell caps. The narrowest end of the stone is fitted into the cap, and it is positioned so that the most attractive facet of the stone faces outwards.

Another type of bell cap has two prongs only. Sometimes referred to as a leaf bail this is the finding to use for suspending a flat stone (fig.2).

Bonding a stone to a bell cap

Choose a bell cap which is of complementary style and in proportionate size to your stone – and into which a corner of the stone will fit sugly. Always test and shape the cap onto the stone before bonding into position.

To ensure that the most attractive facet of the stone is visible in the finished piece of jewelry, turn the bell cap so that the eyelet hole is facing you, and insert the stone with its 'best' face towards you (fig.3). Press the stone down well, making sure that it touches the metal base of the cap. If necessary, lift back the prongs a little with jewelry pliers or tweezers to seat them properly. Press the prongs firmly around the stone again to get the final effect.

Remove the stone and, providing you are satisfied that stone and cap are well suited, proceed to set the stone.

The procedure for attaching a flat stone to a leaf bail type of bell cap is very much the same. Again the question of proportionate size and complementary design should be taken into account. The finding is bent into a U shape the width of the stone. It is then bonded to the stone, leaving a deliberate gap between the top of the U and the stone itself in order to form an eyelet.

Jump rings

Having attached your stone to a bell cap, usually the next step is to pass a jump ring through the bell cap eyelet. Jump rings (fig.2) are round or oval split rings of springy metal which act as connecting links to join one section of jewelry to another. They are used,

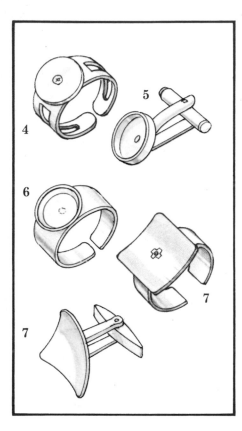

for instance, for hanging a pendant on a neck chain, for drop ear-rings, and for suspending hanging stones from bracelets.

Jump rings are not usually needed for putting a flat stone onto a chain necklet – providing the chain is slim, it can be threaded directly through the U-shaped space left between stone and leaf bail. Most drop ear-ring findings already incorporate a jump ring onto which the bell cap can be directly threaded – so you don't need to add one.

To fix a jump ring

When your stone is firmly secured to its bell cap and the glue has thoroughly dried, open wide a suitable jump ring by twisting both ends of the ring sideways with two pairs of jewelry pliers. Now hook one end of the ring through the eyelet of the bell cap and, if it is to be hung on a loop or link (for an ear-ring, chain bracelet or necklet), thread the other end over the loop or through the link. Then close the jump ring by pinching together firmly with the pliers.

Pad mounts

A large number of ring, brooch, pendant, cufflink, tie pin and ear-ring findings incorporate a pad or pads on which a stone or stones are able to be bonded.

Flat plain pads (fig.4) are probably the easiest for the beginner to use. This is the finding to choose for a stone that has a flat base, and an upper surface (the only part that will show in the completed piece of jewelry) that is attractive and interestingly shaped. Flat pads can be round, oval, square, oblong or triangular, and are available in a good choice of sizes.

It is always best to choose a pad that is as big as possible as this will give your stone maximum support, but remember that the pad must be just small enough to be completely concealed by the stone – or the results will be unsightly.

Large flat pads can be used for mounting a single stone or several smaller ones. Using smaller stones is more tricky because it involves finding stones that harmonize in colour and shape. It also requires considerable care to ensure that the entire area of the pad will be covered. Moreover, because of their size, very small stones or chippings are difficult to handle – but this problem can be minimized by using tweezers or jewelry pliers when applying adhesive and seating the stones into their correct positions.

Flat pads with raised edges (fig.5). Some flat pads – usually round or oval in shape – have raised edges or rims. This edge, which can be plain or decorated, rises at a 90° angle from the pads. These pads

4. Plain flat pad.
5. Flat pad with 90° angle raised edge intended for faceted stones but, if large, can take chippings.
6. Cup pad with flat base and gently raised edge.
7. Concave pads with curved bases are more suited to baroque stones.

are ideal for use with preformed stones and it is really preferable to reserve their use for these stones. Like all pad mounts they can be used for the more irregular shapes of tumbled and polished stones – but be warned that considerable perseverance and luck are needed to search out a suitable candidate stone. It must be flat based and fit precisely into the area. They can also be used for chippings.

Cup pads (fig.6). Again you will have to take care to find a suitable stone but, because the edge rises gently at approximately 135° from the pad, the chances of finding a tumbled stone that fits well are considerably higher.

Concave pads These are dished in varying depths, shapes and sizes to accommodate stones with gently rounded bases (fig.7). Again, it is best to choose a pad which is hidden by your stone but gives it maximum support. Small round filigree concave pads are sometimes called flower pads. They are so decorative that it doesn't matter if the stones fail to completely conceal the pads.

Multi-pads Some findings, notably brooches and rings, incorporate several pads (fig.8). Often these consist of one large pad surrounded by several smaller pads. Or, sometimes, there are several pads of the same size. These are challenging for the jewelry maker intent on using his own tumbled stones because it takes time and patience to assemble stones that make a really attractive set – matching in size and colour and pattern. Moreover, many multi-pads are round or oval in shape and have raised edges – and these should definitely be reserved for use with preformed stones only.

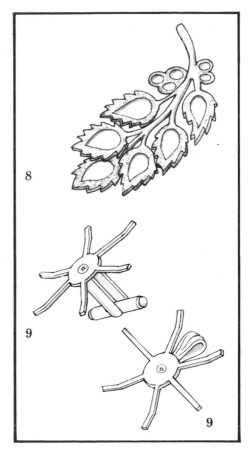

8

9

9

Claw settings

A claw setting is really a cross between a pad mount and a bell cap. It has a central pad onto which part of the stone is bonded, and claws or prongs which can be adjusted to close around the stone and hold it in position (fig.9). A claw setting is the most versatile of the three basic findings, and it can be used for a stone of almost any shape providing the stone has a small flattish area which can be bonded onto the pad. It is very popular setting for rings, brooches and pendants, and increasingly used for cufflink findings and other articles of jewelry too.

How to fit a claw mount Choose a mount of size and style compatible with your stone. Place the stone on it, moving it around until you find the best position. If the stone has any definite bumps, it may be necessary to place each of the bumps between two claws to give a firm grip. Bend the claws gently around the stones with your fingers. Remove the stone and shape each claw with jewelry pliers, then replace the stone and complete the

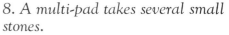

8. *A multi-pad takes several small stones.*
9. *Claw settings are ideal for awkwardly shaped stones.*

87

10. *There are ear-ring findings for pierced and unpierced ears. Choose from (a) butterfly catch, (b) clip, (c) screw, and (d) hook.*

11. *Base metal ring mounts fit any finger size. Different types of adjustable shanks are available as shown in these claw mounts, flat pad and concave pad rings.*

12. *Flat pads and claw mounts are most popular for cufflinks.*

13. *Tie pins, tie tacks and tie clips usually have flat pads.*

14. *Ready made chain bracelets and necklets come in many styles and sizes. Links can be large or small, round, oval, oblong, square or diamond shaped. In a trace chain the links interconnect at right angles. In a curb chain each link is twisted through 90°.*

placement of the claws so that the stone is held in a fairly firm grip. The stone can now be removed again, and the job of cleaning and bonding can begin. Remember that claws must be closely pressed against the stone or they will tend to catch in clothing.

Other jewelry findings

Ear-rings findings These are made for pierced and unpierced ears (fig.10). Check that ear wires are made of sterling silver or gold to avoid inflammation of delicate ear lobes. Drop ear-ring findings usually incorporate a loop onto which bell cap and stone can be threaded direct, but you can add jump rings if you wish to give extra 'dangle' and length.

Obviously, you will wish to spend time and care on selecting stones that look as though they belong together as a pair, but remember that no two stones are ever identical: compatibility of size, shape and colour should be your aim.

Ring mounts The majority of ring mounts have adjustable shanks which can simply be squeezed together to fit any finger (fig.11). But sterling silver and 9ct. gold ring mounts are available in specific finger sizes. They need not be very costly and a silver ring with a flat pad can make an extremely handsome and durable mount for displaying a tumbled stone.

Cufflinks Like ear-rings, cufflinks require compatible stones (fig.12).

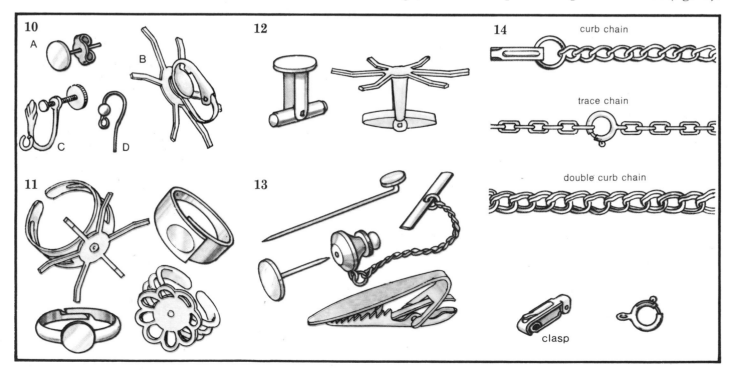

Because cufflinks take a lot of wear, it is particularly important to bond the stones very firmly. Scratching the surface of both stone and pad with a carborundum stone before cleaning and bonding ensures that the adhesive has a good surface to grip on (modern knife sharpeners are usually made of steel but if you have an old fashioned one it is undoubtedly made of carborundum). Some decorative mounts have lacy filigree edges which can be sent over the stone with jewelry pliers for extra security.

Tie pins, tacks and clips Tie pins and tacks nearly always have a small round flat pad (fig.13); and tie clips have a long narrow flat pad onto which a stone or row of stones can be mounted.

Chain bracelet and necklets (fig.14) These can be bought ready made or can be made up by yourself. Trace chains consist of links joined at right angles to each other. In a curb chain each link is twisted through 90° so that the resulting chain has a 'flat look' finish. Chains can be bought purpose made for attaching pendants or hanging stones with bell caps and jump rings, or for threading directly through the gap between a flat stone and a leaf bail. A 68.5cm (27in) chain will slip over the head easily and is therefore a closed chain of links. Anything smaller than a 61cm (24in) chain will include a fastening.

Alternatively, buy a length of chain and a fastening and make the necklet or bracelet yourself. Try to purchase the exact length required. If you have to shorten a chain either open a link (as described for jump rings) and detach the unwanted extra length, or cut through closed metal links with silver shears. Never attempt to do the job with scissors as this will damage both the chain and the scissors.

The most commonly available and simplest type of clasp is a bolt ring. Fit this spring loaded catch to one end of your chain, and a jump ring – onto which the bolt ring can engage – to the other end.

Bracelets and bangles (fig.15) Like cufflinks these are subject to a lot of wear, so it is advisable to use a carborundum stone before applying adhesives. The most usual kind of bracelet mount consists of flat pads joined by links. The pad can be of various shapes and there are usually six to eleven of them. Obviously the greater the number of pads, the more trouble it will take to assemble a set of stones of similar shape and size in harmonizing colours. Occasionally you will find a bracelet mount with several chain links between each pad so that dangling stones can be interspersed with pad bonded stones.

Bangles are usually adjustable wide metal bands with a single large pad. Avoid pads with raised edges unless using chippings or a bought cabochon stone.

15. Bracelet and bangle findings usually have pad mounts. Some findings such as the popular oval flat pad bracelet and the concave flower pad bracelet shown here, are very decorative in their own right so it does not matter if your stones fail to completely cover the pads.

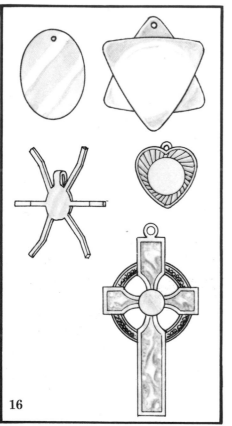

16. A plain pendant is intended to mount and show off a stone. Cast pendants are sometimes ornate enough to wear without a stone.

17. Common types of brooch mounts: narrow bar for a row of stones, oval flat pad for a large stone, bow-shaped fob brooch for bell cap and stone, brooch with decorative outer border and slightly recessed flat pad is suitable for chippings and wreath-shaped brooch with six flat pads for small tumbled stones or preformed stones.

Pendants (fig.16) Basically there are two types of pendant findings, the simple and the ornate. The purpose of a simple pendant is purely to show off a stone. A claw setting falls into this category. So does a small pad which will be completely concealed by the stone.

But the majority of pendant findings are cast mountings and highly decorative in their own right. Available in every imaginable shape and design they incorporate a pad or pads on which a stone can be mounted to complete the ornamentation.

Brooch mounts (fig. 17) can be simple pin backed pads on which a stone or stones can be mounted, or fob brooches (usually in a bow shape) with a loop from which a bell cap and stone can be hung; or decorative cast mounts which incorporate a pad or pads for bonded stones.

Always ensure that a brooch pin is positioned to be above the centre point of your stones–this will avoid the stone tilting forward in an unattractive way. Remember too that looking at the back of the brooch, the pin should always point to the left. Most types are available with a safety catch.

Polished pebble jewelry

Having chosen your stones, polished them and found a suitable mount to match, you can now start to assemble your jewelry pieces. If a lot of care has already gone into preparation and design, this should be the simplest part of the process but care should still be taken to ensure the best possible results.

Making the jewelry

Wash the stones and findings in warm water detergent and, to remove all traces of dirt and grease. Rinse and dry them thoroughly. Even the natural oils from fingers may affect adhesion, so a final wipe over with spirit [turpentine] is a good idea.

Mix the epoxy resin, according to the manufacturer's instructions. Epoxy resin has the advantage of being extremely strong when it is set; but it is correspondingly difficult to remove, so be careful not to let any unwanted traces go hard.

Since the resin takes time to set (up to three days for complete hardening), you may have to hold the stone and finding in position. To do this, pour a quantity of salt, sand or rice into a tray or tin and support them with this. Push the band of a ring or back of a brooch into the sand, so that the surface to be glued stays clear and level.

If you are applying a bell cap to a stone, push the stone in and set the bell cap on it.

Apply the resin with a match-stick to both the finding and the stone. Wipe off any unwanted blobs of glue with a clean rag.

With a 'claw' mount bend the claws into position with jewelry pliers (tweezers may do) before inserting the stone. Pull them out of place as little as possible when inserting the stone and then bend them firmly over it. With a bell cap be careful to position the cap, by watching the position of the eyelet at the top of the cap, so that the face of the stone that you prefer will face outwards when it hangs.

When the glue is dry, brush off any particles of salt or sand from the finding and stone. If the piece needs to be connected to a chain or bracelet do this with a jump ring.

Shell jewelry

The fascinating variety of shells, and their different colours, shapes and textures, make an ideal cheap material for jewelry pieces. As with pebble polishing, there are various levels of involvement; you may just wish to use the shells you have already collected or you may want to clean, polish and colour them or change their shape completely. But, however much you want to involve yourself the techniques are simple and the equipment basic.

Choosing shells

Even if you do not live near the sea, you can collect shells by buying them either direct or by mail order. There are advantages to acquiring shells this way in that there will always be a very wide selection of shells available from all over the world and the shells will already be cleaned and polished for use. If you are using shells you have collected yourself, you can always supplement them with one or two of the more exotic varieties bought from a shop.

Every shell is intrinsically beautiful, however common the species, but when collecting shells for decoration, the most important consideration must be colour, structure and the outline shape of the shell.

You will find that most shells fall into the following categories of shape: spiral (snails such as welks and winkles); cone- or tent-shaped (limpets, top shells); dome-shaped (cockles); flattish (the smooth donax shells which have the quality of very thin porcelain, shiny abalones, and the ridged scallops); spiky (murex shells); smooth and rounded (cowries) and long and pointed (turritellas).

Some of the larger shells, for example abalone shells, can look very effective when broken up into chips and used in pieces. To break up shells, simply put them into a plastic bag and crush them with a hammer. You can buy pieces of abalone for this purpose.

Cleaning shells

To wash the shell use detergent and hot water. Use a toothbrush to brush the smaller shells and a vegetable or nail brush for the larger ones. Make sure that all foreign matter is removed. In order to

Left: Strings of colourful shell beads, used as money by the Solomon islanders.

bleach shells and remove their outside coating (periostracum), soak them in a strong solution of chlorine for a few hours. However, this will discolour coloured shells so use this method only for white shells.

Rinse the shells, dry them thoroughly and polish them with a soft cloth. Wax polish rubbed over a shell will help to bring out its surface pattern and colours. If you prefer, you can apply two coats of clear polyurethane varnish to the shell instead of wax polish.

Piercing

It is very easy to pierce shells with a drill. Most shell drilling is carried out by part-time women workers in a suburb of Naples, Italy. These 'bucatrice' or 'bow drill women' use an archimedean drill, which you can buy from jewelers' supply merchants. It looks like a bow and arrow, with the bow cord twisted around the arrow and shaft holding the shell in the other. The 'bucatrice' work with their coral or shells held in a hand vice fixed to the bench. They are considered to have a much lighter touch with the drill than any male craftsmen.

Small shells, so long as they are not too brittle, can be held between the jaws of a vice to which leather has been stuck.

Large shells will need to be stuck down with lapidary cement (obtainable from lapidary and craft shops). The manner of piercing a shell will depend on the way in which it will lie best in the necklace or with other pieces of jewelry for which it is intended.

Where to drill shells

Generally, the mouth of the shell should always lie on a string so that it is hidden while the jewelry is being worn. A cone shaped shell is often best drilled along its axis from the point of the spire out through the mouth.

Always begin piercing a hole in a shell by making a pilot hole. This is done by twirling a sharp steel tool so as to give the drill some purchase when it begins to bite. It might even be necessary to flatten part of the surface of a shell in an unobtrusive way by rubbing it with a small file before beginning the hole. To pierce a shell take a good quality steel drill bit of about 1mm (1/16in) in thickness (thinner bits can be used but they have a tendency to break). Put the bit in a hand twist drill and drill gently in the hole already formed in the surface of the shell. Go slowly, concentrating on neatness rather than speed.

You can tell by the feel of the drill under your hand when the drill bit has passed through the outer wall of the shell. Once you have gone right through the shell, withdraw the drill slowly, twisting as you go.

Once you have pierced enough shells to make a necklace or other piece of jewelry, arrange them in a row to see how they look. Decide where every individual shell in your collection will show up to best advantage.

Large shells are very suitable for pendants. They do not need to be pierced because they can be suspended simply by cementing to the tip of the cone of the shell a jeweler's finding called a bellcap. This is then attached by means of another finding called a 'jump ring' to a chain. Bracelets can have shells attached by this method, and so can ear-rings.

Spacers

Shell jewelry often looks better when the shells are separated by spacers, which can be turned ivory, wooden beads, nuts or seeds, or mother-of-pearl.

Pieces of mother-of-pearl (see below) can be turned on a lathe or made by cutting oblongs of pearl shell 2.5cm (1in) long by 6mm (¼in) wide.

Make up two square wooden boards, about 30cm by 30cm (12in by 12in) and fix a handle to one of them. Cover one side of each board with wood glue and stick down very coarse sandpaper. Now place the oblongs of mother-of-pearl on top of the sanded side of the bottom board, cover it with the board with the handle attached, and rub the two boards together. It helps if all the oblongs are pointing in the same direction and if you rub the boards at right angles to the long axis of the oblong. Gradually the oblongs will lose their sharp edges and become cylindrical. If some oblongs are hard to smooth, round their edges with a sharp steel file, then sand

Opposite: Some of the many ways in which shells can be threaded as jewelry.
Left: A cowrie shell necklace.
Centre left: An elegant composite design of scallop pendant and whale's teeth on a sequin chain.
Centre right: A string of subtly coloured nerites.
Right: A mushroom coral pendant conbined with precious coral and tusk shells.

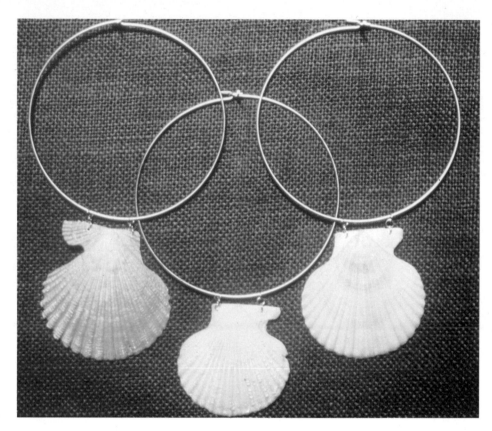

Left: Large shells, such as these scallops, make ideal pendants for chokers. The shells are simply pierced at the top and then attached to the choker band by means of jump rings.

Opposite: Long string necklaces.
Far left: Moon snails with pearl spacers.
Left: A string of dove shells.

with medium and fine sandpaper.

Drill through the finished oblongs (which are called 'bangles') along their axis. Drill from both ends and let the holes meet in the middle.

Square pieces of mother-of-pearl can be converted into round spacers by moving the two boards in a circular direction as you rub.

Stripping and polishing shells

Many shells have a shiny interior coating of nacre, which is better known as mother-of-pearl. This substance is composed of the same silvery, shimmering material as pearls, but whereas pearls are very rare and therefore precious, mother-of-pearl can be obtained in large quantities and is one of the cheapest of all jewelry materials. Stripping can be done in various ways. Small shells are simply left to steep in a solution of household bleach and water, in a proportion of one part bleach to four parts water, until the acid in the bleach eats away the blue-black outside layer of the shell and reveals the silvery underside of the mother-of-pearl. It takes a day or two for the outside coat (periostracum) to disappear. Leave the shells in

the solution in a glass jar and inspect them from time to time to see how the stripping is progressing.

Once the periostracum has been removed, the shells should be well washed, first in a little liquid soap and water, then in clear water, to remove all traces of bleach.

Grinding will remove the periostracum of thicker shells. If an old-fashioned grindstone is available, you can force the shell against its edge while someone else turns the grinder, but a quicker way is to use a small grindstone attachment in the chuck [shell] of an electric drill.

First cement the shell to a bench, using dop cement (lapidary cement). Melt the cement over a wax taper or candle until it is fluid, then dab the bench and the bottom of the shell with it. Stick the shell to the bench while the cement is still sticky. When the cement has cooled, the shell should stick firmly to the bench.

Work the grindstone in the drill slowly over the surface of the shell. Avoid cutting too deeply or making score marks. When you have ground away as much as you can with the grindstone, fit an abrasive head into a flexible drive and grind into all the small crevices.

Lever the shell off the bench with a screwdriver. When you have ground one part, stick it down in another position, then grind again. When the whole outside layer has been removed and the nacre is shining over the whole surface of the shell, stripping is complete and the shell can be polished.

Some shells, such as top shells and nautili, have such thin layers of periostracum that it is inadvisable to strip them mechanically, but they can be stripped with an alabaster knife, as used by sculptors and obtainable from sculptor's tool merchants. This looks like a miniature scimitar, except that its curved blade has a sharp edge on both sides. Sharpen both edges well with a whetstone and cradle the shell firmly between the knees with enough pressure to hold it without breaking it.

Hold the knife by the point with the left hand and the handle with the right and scrape delicately at the outside covering, using the inside of the knife blade to fit snugly around the curve of the shell. Other sharp craft knives with disposable blades can also be used, and a razor blade in a safety holder will strip any awkward patches. Shells can also be rubbed down, first with a coarse, then with medium and fine sandpaper, and then polished.

Splitting shells

Shells can be split down the middle to show all the little chambers inside. This is usually done by professional shell craftsmen who use a lapidary wheel, but there is no reason why this should not be attempted at home.

Choose a fairly small shell. Cement one side to a board with dop cement. Clamp the board in a vice.

Make a cut along the top of the shell with a triangular-shaped file to start the saw cut. With a 2.5cm (1in) wide metal piercing blade in a hack saw, cut very gently through the nautilus, lubricating the blade with water as you go.

Instead of cutting straight through the shell make a pencil line first and cut along the line from two directions so that the cuts meet.

Lay the two halves on a sheet of fine sandpaper and rub them gently on it until the cut edges are smooth.

Polishing

A stripped shell has to be polished after stripping to bring out its beauty to the full. Rub first with finest flour sandpaper (usually 'O'). Then rub it with a wet cotton rag dipped in powdered pumice.

Right: Fragile shells should be stripped manually, using an alabaster knife.

Keep rubbing until a shine begins to show. Wipe off every trace of the polishing powder, dip another rag in the powder and polish afresh.

Finally rub the shell with a wet rag dipped in a tablespoon of copper sulphate dissolved in a cupful of warm water.

A coat of clear lacquer or embedding the shells in clear cast plastic resin will preserve iridescence.

Painting and dyeing

Shells can be painted with enamel paint sold for military miniatures. Before painting, clean the shell with a rag dipped in turpentine, then paint, preferably not over the entire surface but with a design which will allow the beautiful designs on the shell background to show through.

Gilt can be applied by painting a design on a shell with Japan gold size (tinted to show up against a white shell). Press gold leaf onto the size while it is still tacky [sticky], allowing it to dry hard, then gently brush off the residue of leaf with a stiff brush before burnishing smooth with a stone such as blood stone.

Jewelry from plastics

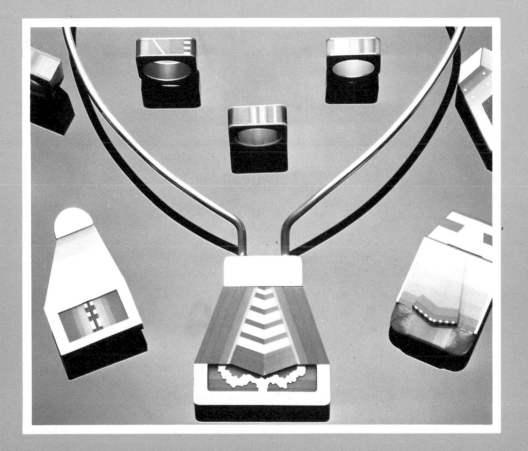

Types of plastic

Plastic is a lightweight material that comes in an exciting variety of forms and colours and is very easily worked. It is often considered solely as a substitute for materials such as glass, wood or metal but, in fact, it has properties that make it totally unique as a crafts material.

It is made up from chemicals derived from coal and petroleum and this chemical structure can be altered to suit different purposes.

Plastic is really a collective word for a number of materials, many quite unlike one another. However, they can by divided into two main groups.

Thermoplastics

These are plastics which are hard at normal temperature but soften when heated. The material can then be shaped and moulded and will retain the new shape when it cools to its former solid mass. This process can be repeated a number of times before the material starts to break down so that if you make a mistake, it can be corrected.

Acrylic in sheets, celluloid, polystyrene and polyvinyl acetate (PVA) are all example of thermoplastics.

Thermosetting plastics

These are a group of material that undergo a chemical change which is irreversible. They solidify in the presence of heat and, once shaped and cooled, they cannot be reworked.

Polyester resins are thermosetting plastics. They have a syrup-like consistency and, when mixed with a catalyst – the hardener – they generate heat and cool down to a solid. Resins are made for different applications so always make sure that the resin you use is suitable for the particular job you are doing. Resins for clear casting are especially made to remain clear with little or no optical distortion. These are also treated to avoid excessive shrinkage so that when a solid object is embedded in them they will not crack around the object. Polyester resin is easy to work with and is suitable for craft purposes in the home.

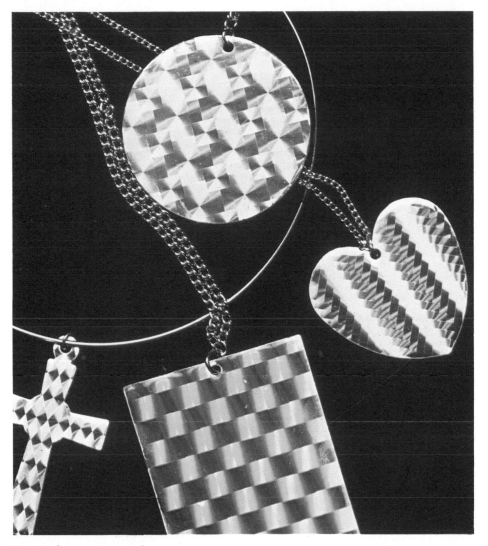

Left: Simple pendants made using defraction foil. Bought as a sheet, the grooves break up the light to create rainbow colours.

Rainbow jewelry
You will need : Defraction foil is sold by length from a roll and is 15cm (6in) wide. Metal blank (drilled with a hole for a pendant, without for a pin). Clear general-purpose glue.

Rainbow jewelry

The shimmering rainbow effect of these pendants is created by defraction foil. This is, in fact, a thin silvery plastic sheet that has had very fine grooves cut into it, rather like those on a record, in a pattern. The grooves break up light into rainbow colours in the manner of a prism. To cover a wall with this material would be expensive but a small piece will go along way in making jewelry.

To mount the foil on a metal blank, cut a piece of foil slightly larger than the shape you are using.

Glue the foil onto the metal blank with a clear, general purpose glue. Leave to dry and then very carefully trim away excess foil with a sharp knife. Thread onto a chain or silken cord to make a pendant or glue the blank onto a brooch fitting.

Jewelry from acrylic sheet

Attractive and colourful jewelry can easily and cheaply be made from small pieces of acrylic which are available from most acrylic suppliers. The principle involved is the same as for all thermoplastics in that heat is applied to the material which can then be shaped and moulded to the desired design.

Shaping

It is necessary to heat the whole piece of acrylic. This is done by placing the acrylic on a flat surface, such as a piece of aluminium foil in a baking tray, and putting the tray in a medium oven – about 66°C (150°F), gas mark 4 – for ten minutes until the acrylic is very soft and pliable. The acrylic is then removed and wrapped around a cylinder of the appropriate diameter to make a bangle or ring. While still around the cylinder, the acrylic is placed in a dish of cold water to cool and harden it.

The surface of the acrylic may have become slightly distorted during this process, and you will find that the outside edges will have curled up slightly. This can easily be remedied by sanding them down with very fine silicon carbide paper and water to produce a smooth, matt finish.

Any bangle or ring made using this method will, of course, have a small gap where the two ends meet. This makes the bangle or ring slightly flexible and easier to put on.

One great advantage of working with acrylic is that it has what is called 'plastic memory' which means that if you make a bangle to the wrong shape, you can place it back in a hot oven for the same amount of time and the acrylic will return to its original shape.

Laminating

In order to produce stripes of colour, or to let one colour 'glow' through another, pieces of acrylic are stuck together using a special acrylic glue.

It is possible to shape two pieces of acrylic that have been stuck together to make a striped bangle, but unless the pieces are stuck properly, and held together in a vice while setting, they will come apart during heating. When laminating with transparent acrylic the glue must be applied on areas that will not show since the glue distorts the surface of the acrylic.

Sanding

Acrylic sheet is sanded using silicon carbide paper and water. To ensure that the sanded surface of the acrylic will be flat, the silicon carbide paper is first of all stuck to a sheet of glass with double-sided tape and the acrylic rubbed against this.

When sanding the inside of curved surfaces the silicon carbide paper should be wrapped around a piece of dowel.

In order to produce a smooth matt finish the acrylic must be sanded with very fine silicon carbide paper and with very small circular movements. The surfaces can be polished with metal polish.

Most of the acrylic that can be bought as scrap is the standard thickness of about 3mm ($\frac{1}{8}$in). However, thinner pieces can be made by sanding down on one side to the required thickness.

Striped bracelet

The blue bracelet is made of two layers of differently coloured acrylic stuck on each side of a central layer.

Below left: Trace pattern for the striped bracelet. Cut two sets of shapes and one complete ring.

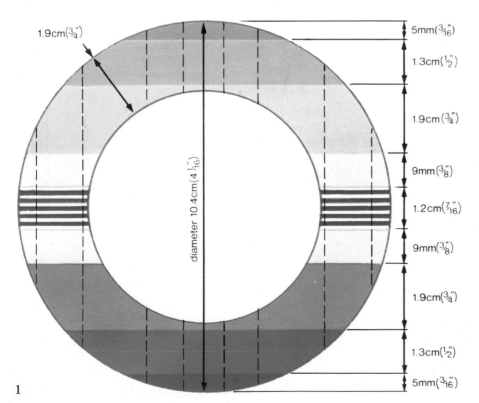

1.9cm($\frac{3}{4}$")

diameter 10.4cm(4$\frac{1}{16}$")

5mm($\frac{3}{16}$")
1.3cm($\frac{1}{2}$")
1.9cm($\frac{3}{4}$")
9mm($\frac{3}{8}$")
1.2cm($\frac{7}{16}$")
9mm($\frac{3}{8}$")
1.9cm($\frac{3}{4}$")
1.3cm($\frac{1}{2}$")
5mm($\frac{3}{16}$")

1

Striped bracelet

You will need:
Acrylic in the following colours and sizes:
Green and navy blue 1.3cm × 5cm ($\frac{1}{2}$in × 2in).
Royal blue 2.5cm × 8.5cm (1in × 3$\frac{1}{4}$in).
Pale turquoise and mid blue 10.5cm × 4cm (4$\frac{1}{4}$in × 1$\frac{5}{8}$in).
Pale blue 4.4cm × 4cm (1$\frac{3}{4}$in × 1$\frac{5}{8}$in).
White and black 3cm × 2.5cm (1$\frac{1}{4}$in × 1in).
Turquoise 13.2cm × 10.5cm (5$\frac{1}{4}$in × 4$\frac{1}{4}$in).
Acrylic glue.
Silicon carbide paper, medium and fine.
Piece of glass about 30cm (12in) square.
G-clamp [C-clamp].
Drill with a 6mm ($\frac{1}{4}$in) bit.
Small piece of wood.
Piercing saw or coping saw with very fine blade.
Paper and wax pencil.
Piece of dowel.
Metal polish.
Double-sided tape.

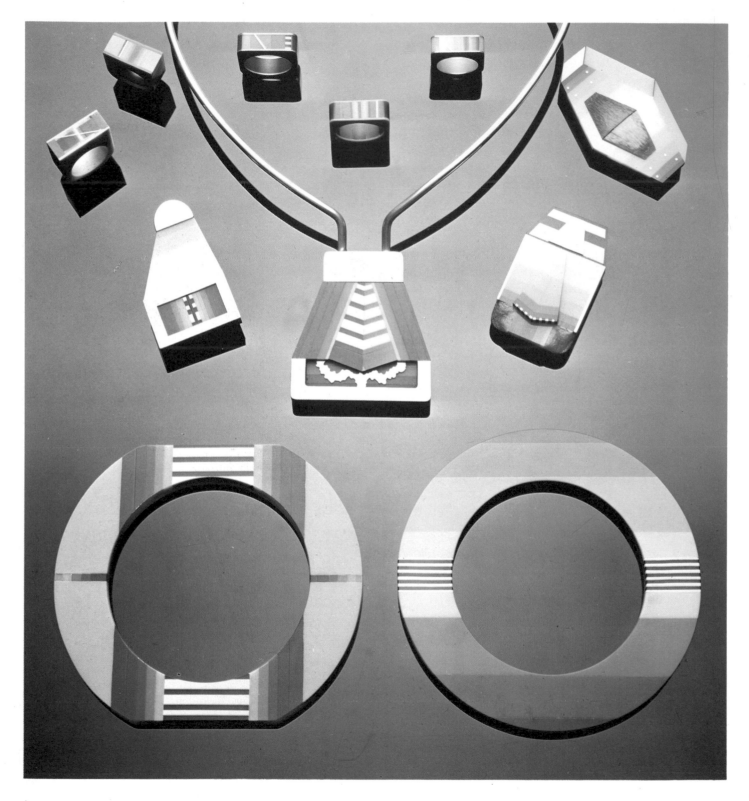

Enlarge the pattern pieces in fig.1 to the measurements given. If the acrylic still has the protective paper on it, draw the shapes onto this. If not draw the pattern shapes onto the surface of the acrylic with a wax pencil (this can be rubbed off later).

The black and white striped areas could be made from two solid pieces of white and two of black acrylic as cutting strips of less than 2mm ($\frac{1}{16}$in) wide is difficult.

Use a piercing saw (fig.2) to cut out two sets of the shapes shown in fig.1, and one solid bracelet shape (this should be cut from the turquoise). When using the piercing saw, cut on the downward stroke and use long strokes to avoid overheating the blade.

Opposite: Acrylic sheet can be used to make a wide variety of attractive jewelry pieces. Using the basic techniques, rings, pendants and colourful bangles can all be worked.

Below: Simple shaping techniques are used to make this brilliant red matching bracelet and ring.

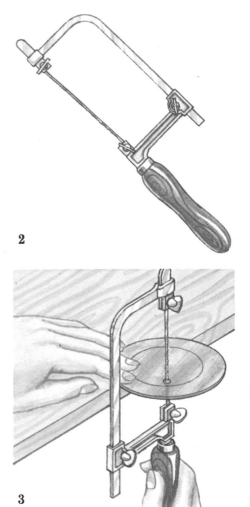

2

3

2. A piercing saw for cutting
acrylic.
3. Drill a hole and insert the
blade.

Above right: Shaping the acrylic.
Place the heated acrylic strip
along the line drawn on the paper.

To cut out the inside of the bangle, secure acrylic in G-clamp [C-clamp] protecting it with a piece of wood, and drill a hole in the waste area of the acrylic disc, undo one end of the saw, slot the blade of the piercing saw through the hole and do it up again (fig.3).

Following fig.1, stick one set of shapes onto one side of the solid turquoise shape using the acrylic glue. Turn the bracelet over and stick the other set of shapes on the other side as indicated with a dotted line in fig.1. You may find that the different coloured pieces of acrylic are not exactly the same thickness. This will be evened out in the final sanding.

Stick a piece of medium silicon carbide paper to the piece of glass with double sided tape. Sand down the two sides of the bracelet by rubbing onto the silicon carbide paper.

Sand the inside edge of the bracelet with a piece of silicon carbide paper wrapped around a piece of dowel.

Next sand all the edges with the fine silicon paper in the same way. This will result in a smooth, matt finish. If you wish to polish the acrylic further use a metal polish.

Bangles and rings

These are made using the shaping technique discussed at the beginning of this chapter.

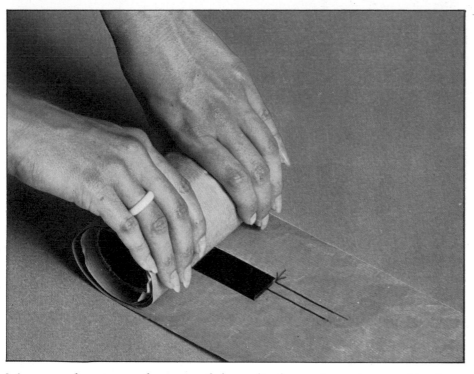

Left: Roll the paper and acrylic around the cylinder to make the bangle.

Measure the circumference of the cylinder and cut the acrylic about 3mm ($\frac{1}{8}$in) shorter than this.

Secure the acrylic in a G-clamp [C-clamp] and cut to the required length, and as wide as you want the bangle to be.

Meanwhile, heat the oven to about 66°C (150°F), gas mark 4.

Place the cut piece of acrylic on the aluminium foil on a baking tray and place in the oven for about ten minutes.

Draw a line lengthways on the paper.

Test that the acrylic is soft enough by lifting one corner with the point of a knife. It should be very soft and pliable. If blisters appear on the surface of the acrylic, the oven is too hot.

Wearing the asbestos gloves remove the acrylic from the oven and place on the piece of paper along the line. Place the cylinder at right angles to the acrylic and start to roll the paper and the acrylic around the cylinder with the piece of acrylic sandwiched between the cylinder and paper.

Immerse the cylinder, acrylic and paper in a dish of cold water to cool and harden the acrylic.

Take the acrylic bangle out and sand down as for the bracelet.

If the bangle has not turned out well, replace in the oven, heat up again until the acrylic has regained its original shape and try again.

Rings can be made in the same way using a cylinder with a smaller diameter.

Bangles and rings

You will need:
Acrylic sheet scraps about 30cm (12in) long for the bangles and about 5cm (2in) long for the rings and as wide as you like.
G-clamp [C-clamp] and hacksaw.
Silicon carbide paper, medium and fine grade.
Metal polish.
Two cylindrical formers of suitable diameter such as biscuit tins or dowelling to make bracelet and rings.
Pieces of stiff paper and pencil.
Gas or electric oven.
Asbestos gloves.
Sheet of aluminium foil and baking tray.
Dish of water.
Tape measure.

Jewelry from resin

Polyester resins are thermosetting plastics from which you can make beautiful jewelry in all kinds of intricate shapes. The resin flows into a mould made by a metal strip and glass, sequins, wire, glitter and small beads can be embedded in it. When cured the resin can be finished in a number of different ways to give you jewelry which is both attractive and durable.

To make jewelry

The materials given below are sufficient to make all the pendants shown here. Since the quantities are so small, you should stock up on the full amount even though you may only want to make one pendant. If you do this you will have enough materials to allow for any mistakes or to make several pieces of jewelry.

To make a pendant

Work in a warm, well-ventilated room and set out all the tools and materials you will need on a drawing board or flat, hard surface.

Using the tin snips or scissors, cut a length of metal strip and bend it into the shape of the pendant. The metal is very flexible but start by making a simple outline, the more intricate design details can be added inside. For a circular pendant, a more regular shape can be formed by moulding the strip around a coin or piece of wooden dowel of a suitable diameter. Glue the ends of the strip together with the adhesive and leave to dry. For the different coloured sections within the pendant, cut out strips of metal to fit tightly inside the pendant to act as resin dividers. There is no need to glue these strips.

Take the plastic or cellophane sheet and cut it in half. Place one half on the drawing board or flat surface and tape the edges down making sure that the sheet is flat and taut.

Place the metal outline of the pendant onto the plastic sheet and tape the strip to the drawing board by stretching the tape across the pendant from one side of the board to the other (fig.1). If you are making a small pendant the tape may completely cover the metal outline so, cut a notch into the tape where it covers the metal strip.

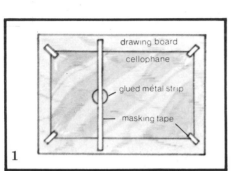

1. *Having decided the design of your pendant, place the metal strip outline on the cellophane and stretch the tape across the pendant from one side of the board to the other.*

Opposite: Pendants made using different colour pigments. These should be added in the second layer of resin with any objects to be embedded.

First layer Mix up 28gm (1oz) of resin with eight drops of catalyst and gently pour into the pendant to make the first layer of clear resin. A needle can be used to guide the resin when pouring it. The resin should just cover the bottom surface but should not be more than 3mm (⅛in) deep. A little resin may seep under the metal strip but this can be removed later. Leave the resin to cure in a warm room for two or three hours until it has gelled.

Second layer Mix up another 28gm (1oz) resin with catalyst. This second layer of resin contains the colours in the pendant, so divide it up into tins for the number of colours desired. To control the colour, add the pigment in small quantities to each tin. You can then add more if the colour is not deep enough.

Very gently pour the resin into the sections formed by the metal strips inside the pendant. This is a painstaking job and needs to be done carefully.

If the pendant is to contain small chips of glass, foil, beads or

The pendant

You will need :
220gm (½lb) clear embedding resin.
Small bottle of catalyst. (This usually comes in a 56gm (2oz) size and you will need less than half of this quantity.)
Resin pigments in red, blue and green. You will only need a very small quantity depending on the depth of colour required.
Aluminium [aluminum], brass or copper strip about 8mm (5/16 in) wide and 90cm (3ft) long. This is a very thin, flexible strip used to make a mould for the resin.
Silver-plated, brass or copper wire about 0.6mm (gauge 22-23) thick. You will only need 30cm (1ft) for making the pendants, more if you intend to suspend the pendants from the wire.
Thin jewelry chains for suspending the pendants if you are not using wire for this purpose.
Epoxy adhesive.
Thin polyester sheet, preferably transparent, or thickish cellophane paper, 90cm × 90cm (3ft × 3ft).
Calibrated disposable cups for measuring.
Small tins for mixing resin.
Tin snips or heavy duty scissors.
Smooth stick or spatula for mixing resin.
Masking tape.
Medium-size needle.
Flat, smooth piece of wood about 15cm × 15cm (6in × 6in), or a hardback book.
Resin or metal polish.
Medium glasspaper [sandpaper], medium and fine wet and dry silicon carbide paper (for opaque finish).
Polyurethane varnish (optional).
Hand drill and small bit (optional).

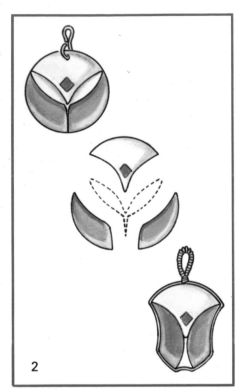

2

Top: Separate the resin sections to make a completely different pendant.
Above: Translucent resin butterfly pendant.

sequins, add them to the second layer of resin after you have poured it into the various sections.

At this stage do not completely fill the pendant with resin. Leave a small space for 'topping up'. As the resin cures it will naturally shrink very slightly and you will have room for a third layer.

If the first layer of resin has seeped under the bottom edge of the metal strip you can lift it away with the point of the needle. This should be done before it has time to harden.

Third layer When the second layer has gelled, mix up another 28gm (1oz) of resin with catalyst and pour on top of the second layer. This third clear layer finishes the pendant and should reach the top of the metal strip.

Place a small piece of plastic sheet across the top of the resin so that it touches the entire surface. Smooth the sheet gently with your finger to release any air bubbles that could be trapped underneath. Weight the sheet with a board or book. This combination of sheet and board will aid the curing process and ensure that the pendant has a flat, smooth surface.

You may find that a little resin has dribbled over the top of the mould. This is nothing to worry about. Let the pendant harden overnight.

When the pendant has cured, prise away the outside metal strip which will have got a little messy by this time. You can leave the pendant without a band or you can cut another strip, wind it around the edge of the resin and glue as before.

Polishing The surface of the resin should be quite smooth and only needs a rub with a resin or metal polish to bring up the shine. Alternatively, you may like to obtain frosted opaque finish. In this case, sand down the resin with medium glasspaper [sandpaper], followed by medium and fine wet and dry paper.

The sanding will also remove any stickiness left on the surface of the resin.

Varnishing

The pendant can also be varnished with a polyurethane varnish which will cover any stickiness and slight unevenness in the resin. The varnish, however, does not give such a good shine as a smoothly polished surface.

If the pendant encloses two or three metal strips (used as resin dividers) the various sections of the pendant can be separated as in fig.2. You may find that the sections can be rearranged in a number of ways and then held in place by a length of metal wire.

To hang the pendant, cut a small piece of wire to make a loop and stick to the top of the pendant with adhesive.

Cold enamelling techniques

The traditional art of enamelling has been practised for at least two thousand years and may have originated in Western Europe: early Greek writers describe the colourful designs of the enamel-decorated weapons and armour used by northern barbarians.

In early examples of Greek and Celtic enamel work, only opaque enamels were used, and it was not until the 12th century that glowing, translucent colours appeared in the work of the Gothic enamellers. The craft gradually developed and fine examples were produced by the jewelers of Elizabethan England and in France in the 18th century. By the early 20th century, the enamellers of the Russian firm of Carl Faberge were producing work of incredible precision and technique. In recent years, the art of enamelling has enjoyed a revival and artists are again using techniques which have not changed basically for many thousands of years.

Enamel effects with resin

Fine enamelling can only be done on objects that can withstand the heat necessary for the process. Modern developments, however, mean that the effect of enamelling can be applied to wood, paper or plastics that would not survive being heated in a kiln, as well as metals and glass. Cold enamelling, as the process is called, can be used on almost any surface.

The basis of cold enamelling is a cold-setting liquid plastic. To this, in its liquid form, various pigments are added for colouring: these can be opaque or translucent and other special effects are available, such as metallic and fluorescent colours. The plastic, which comes in two parts, is mixed first, then the colouring is added and the liquid is applied to the surface and left to dry.

There are introductory kits available for cold enamelling. These typically include the two-part plastic, a variety of pigments, metal blanks and findings for making brooches, pendants, cufflinks and ear-rings. They also include aluminium foil dishes for mixing, mixing sticks, measuring beaker, spoon, brush and cleaning fluid, as well as the manufacturer's instructions. Once you have used a kit, however, you will want to buy particular materials separately

Right: Some of the things you can easily decorate with cold enamel. If you are decorating a pair of cuff-links, for example, with the random technique, they do not turn out identical but this can be really effective, as long as you use colours carefully to give an impression of matching.

as you need them: there's no point in paying twice for packaging and measuring beakers.

Instead of cold enamelling materials, clear-cast resin can be used, but the amount of recommended catalyst should be increased to cure the surface.

Preparations

Liquid plastic will adhere firmly to the surface onto which it is applied, and although it can be removed while it is still in liquid form it is best to avoid the problem. So, before embarking on cold enamelling, prepare your work area by covering it with protective layers of newspaper or plastic sheeting.

The liquid plastic has a slight odour. This is not unpleasant but it is advisable to have some ventilation. A warm, dust-free room gives the best working conditions. The warmth helps the finished enamelling to set more quickly and the less dust there is in the atmosphere, the higher the gloss on the finished piece will be.

Be careful not to confuse the two separate containers which hold the liquid plastic and the hardener – when the two liquids are mixed, they set into solid plastic. So, if you put the wrong top on the containers, you may never be able to open them again. The containers are made to be distinctive to guard against this possibility.

As with all crafts, a beginner is advised to experiment initially with small quantities, using cardboard or other scrap material.

Preparing the plastic

Pour 10ml (2 teaspoons) of liquid plastic and 5ml (1 teaspoon) of the hardener into the measuring jug. This amount will do for your first attempts; later, judge for yourself how much you will need, but always use the proportion of two parts plastic to one part hardener. Mix the liquid thoroughly together and pour it into two or more of the foil dishes.

Add a different colour to each dish, mixing the colours thoroughly into the liquid as you add them. Use as little pigment as possible, since too much will cause the plastic to take longer to set. For best results, you will need to use rather more of the opaque colours than the translucent ones.

It takes very little practice to judge how much pigment you need. Make sure that the solution will remain workable for between two and three hours at normal room temperature.

Applying the plastic

There are two basic techniques for using the cold enamel solutions – you can mix two or more colours in a liquid state or allow one colour to set hard before adding subsequent layers. The first technique requires careful choice of colours and some skill but there is an element of chance in the way in which the colours swirl together which can be most pleasing.

Mixing liquid colours Select the background colour and apply this over the whole area to be enamelled, using a small paintbrush or mixing stick. Next, drip a small amount of a second colour onto the still liquid base and watch how the two colours run together. For a more varied effect follow this with a third colour. But beware of using too many different colours as they may clash or give too cluttered a design.

A further interesting variation can be achieved by running a toothpick or needle through the pattern, which often produces an attractive, swirling effect. A little experimentation will show you how to mix the colours and how much they tend to run into each other.

Hardening between layers By allowing one coat to set hard before applying another, you can achieve full control of the colours you apply. In this way you can demonstrate your own skill in decoration and design. If you have completely covered the surface

with the first coat, subsequent coats will be in relief on the first coat and you can use this property to emphasize the design.

Using half-set plastic If you are working with a detailed design – and even more if you are working on a rounded or non-horizontal surface – you will find it easier to control the flow of the plastic if you allow it to harden a little before applying it. The plastic starts to set as soon as the two parts are mixed and the longer you wait the less fluid it becomes. You will need to experiment to find out when the plastic is suitably viscous for use on a curved surface or where you do not want it to run.

If you find that the top surface of the plastic, after application, is not perfectly smooth, don't worry. Although any movement may be almost imperceptible, the plastic will remain liquid enough for several hours to eliminate any dents in the surface.

When covering a flat surface, you may want to build up a thick coat of enamel without letting it run down the edge of the surface. On small, flat brooches and other pieces of jewelry, on which you are applying a thin coat, surface tension will be enough to hold the plastic. When applying the plastic near the edge, treat it gently and it will dry to a neatly curved, smooth edge.

If the layer of plastic is too thick to allow this, use adhesive tape to build a 'wall' around the edge, to hold the plastic in. When the plastic has completely hardened, remove the tape. You will find a rough edge, raised from the overall surface. Smooth this off with fine abrasive paper – you may need to smooth some tape off this way too, if it has stuck too hard. The finer the paper you use, the better the finish. Finally polish the edge.

Polishing

You can polish an edge by applying a very thin layer of uncoloured plastic. This is liable to cause the same difficulties as before with the edge, but if you use the plastic half-set it will probably work. This method is best if there are scratch marks to cover up.

For polishing in general, use a liquid metal polish and a rag. This will shine up an edge or restore the shine to any cold-enamelled piece which has become dull.

Hardening

It takes several days for the plastic to harden completely but it is usually too solid to be workable about three hours after it is mixed. Once you have applied the plastic, the object should be left in a warm, dust-free place. After about 24 hours, the plastic should be set enough to be handled carefully. It will continue to harden for several days, especially if a thick coat has been applied. When fully hardened, it is extremely durable.

Reluctance to harden may be due to the application of too much pigment. But the plastic will set eventually – patience and a warm place are all that is required. It is inadvisable to try to speed up the initial hardening process by using more hardener than is recommended or by using high temperatures.

Safety hints

Treated properly, cold enamelling is perfectly safe. Any fumes given off by the plastic or pigment are not toxic or inflammable but the materials themselves will burn if a direct flame is applied to them. They should on no account be eaten or drunk. Keep the material away from food and from your eyes.

Sensitive skin may be irritated by contact with the plastic. Try not to touch it but, if any does get on your skin, wash it off at once with warm, soapy water.

Finally, since the plastic does stick hard to most surfaces when it sets, wipe it off with an old rag if any spills. Wrap the rag up, to prevent the plastic from spreading, and throw it away. Mixing containers can similarly be wiped and later re-used.

Below: Many of the effects of traditional enamelling techniques can be achieved using cold enamels. This pendant is made using the cloisonné technique. Simply bend thin metal wire into the shape of the design you want and stick it to the surface of the blank using a thin coat of clear plastic. When this has set, paint coloured cold enamel into each compartment.

Jewelry
from scraps

Feather motif

Since earliest times, feathers have had an immense appeal for man. Their shimmering colours and wonderful variety of textures and shape have captivated the eye and excited the imagination and a wealth of ingenious ornamentation has resulted. Here we show you one of the ways in which smaller feathers can be used to make a brooch but, with a little skill larger projects can be worked.

Types of feathers

All sizes and types of feather can be used in some way and the types of feathers present on a single bird vary considerably. Basically, there are the big, strong, flat wing and tail feathers, the softer body feathers which follow the contours of the body, curving one way on one side of the body, and the opposite way on the other, and there are the short curly neck feathers. Many subdivisions exist as well because feathers vary in colour and markings as well as shape. There are 34 different types of feathers on the duck alone and often colouring is deceptive. On the Rhode Island Red chicken, for instance, there are snow white feathers which are completely out of view, showing only chestnut tips which create the overall colour of the bird.

Sources of feathers

Many countries, such as England, have restrictions about the importation of feathers from wild birds and these help to preserve them from commercial exploitation. However, there are a number of readily available sources of feathers and searching for them can be an adventure in itself. It is worth noting here that under no condition should you ever try to extract a feather from a live bird. Zoo grounds, farmyards or even a friendly butcher or poulterer are all good sources for both domestic and exotic feathers, while shops and florists often sell feathers particularly ostrich plumes and those most spell binding of all, the tail feathers of the peacock. These are available because ostriches are clipped and peacocks moult their tail feathers annually; thus their feathers become available to the public with no harm to the birds.

Feather motif

The motif illustrated, made of goose and pheasant feathers, shows the basic assembly of feathers to make a design. It would look equally well on a lapel or hatband and although the feathers shown are in their natural colours, others can be used and dyed beforehand.

Dyeing feathers is amazingly easy to do. Use hot water dye and make sure the feathers are completely submerged. Move them around in the dye for one minute to ensure that the water resistance of the feathers is penetrated.

Make a small flat oval of adhesive putty slightly larger than your thumb and press the feathers into it in the following order: Begin with the satin goose feather; trim it first with scissors to about 8cm (3in) long, cutting as much as possible to each snip. Place this feather beneath the putty so it will hide it on the underside.

Then press the long red spur feather into the putty so that the top extends well beyond the first feather.

Next press the pheasant 'church window' then 3 pheasant back feathers, followed by the 4 gold sides. Position the first row at the top of the putty and work down, overlapping the feathers as you go so that each one can be pressed into the putty surface. Add 3 more pheasant back feathers and complete by adding 3 pheasant neck feathers spread out in a fan shape.

To make a fastener use ordinary glue and dab it to a pin fastener and press this to the central shaft of the first feather.

Right: The feather motif is composed mainly of pheasant feathers and can be used to decorate a hat or a lapel.

Feather motif

You will need :
1 satin goose feather.
1 red spur from a pheasant's tail.
1 pheasant 'church window' feather.
6 pheasant back feathers.
4 pheasant gold sides.
3 pheasant neck feathers.
Adhesive putty.
Scissors.
Pin fastener.

Horseshoe nail necklaces

Horseshoe nails may seem out of place anywhere but in a stable, but they lend themselves to making jewelry as they are made from stainless steel and have an interesting design. The jewelry, consisting of horseshoe nails combined with wire and perhaps a leather thong, can be fairly heavy so, although designs are limitless, do not use too many nails on any one piece. Generally, bracelets can be fairly heavy but necklaces and pendants – anything worn around the neck – should be of a comfortable weight.

Buying horseshoe nails

The nails can be bought from a blacksmith or ironmonger [hardware store] and are sold by weight. They are available in various sizes so if you are only buying a small quantity try to get a selection of at least three different sizes.

Sizes of nails vary and a blacksmith [hardware store] might not stock all the different sizes. The sizes used for the jewelry shown here vary between sizes 2 and 8. To avoid confusion with size numbers and suitable alternatives, sizes 2-4 will be referred to as small, sizes 5-6 as medium, sizes 7-8 as large. Try to buy the nails in alternate sizes, for example, 3,5,7, or 4, 6, 8.

Technique

Note that the nails are slightly irregular in shape. The side with the trademark on it has a sloping end towards the point. Always combine the nails in any particular design with the trademark in the same position or alternate them but do not use them haphazardly as this will unbalance a design.

The horseshoe nails are curled with round-nosed pliers and joined together or attached by wire. You may find it difficult at first to bend the nails, however a little practice will strengthen the fingers. The nail tip must be bent in two stages. First, the very pointed tip of the nail must be curled. Use the front end of a pair of round-nosed pliers to curl the end slightly to begin the curve. Then move the pliers up from the end of the nail and complete the curl. Bend

Below: Beads used with horseshoe nails should have a hole large enough to fit the nails.

Right: An effective, balanced design using horseshoe nails and beads. When designing necklaces of this type, remember that it should be of a comfortable weight.

The necklace with beads

You will need:
Wire cutters.
Round-nosed pliers.
Household or combination pliers.
Materials:
42cm (16½in) long 1.4mm (gauge 15-17) nickel silver wire.
61cm (24in) long, 0.8mm (gauge 20-21) nickel silver wire.
2 small and 3 medium sized horse-shoe nails.
24 red beads, 5 yellow beads.

---

all the nails like this, one small curve to start and then the next curve to finish and try to do the second stage with one turn of the wrist. This will help to get even curls leaving only minor adjustments when you assemble the jewelry. To make it easier you can heat the nails over a flame (a gas cooker [stove] is ideal for this) and then when they are red-hot, bend to the required shape.

The heat will discolour the nails but it does not make them unattractive – in fact the mottled blue-grey effect can be very pretty. To heat a nail, grip the thick end securely with a pair of household pliers held in the left hand and hold the pointed end of the nail over the flame. When the nail is red-hot, take it away from the flame and, using the round-nosed pliers in the right hand, quickly bend the nail. You can re-heat it if necessary to complete the curl.

The necklace with beads

The necklace has a circumference of 40cm (15¾in) and will fit around an average-sized neck.

If nickel silver wire is unobtainable you can substitute tinned-copper, galvanized iron wire, silver-plated copper wire or mild steel. Try to find wire that is not too difficult to handle and of a colour suited to that of the nails.

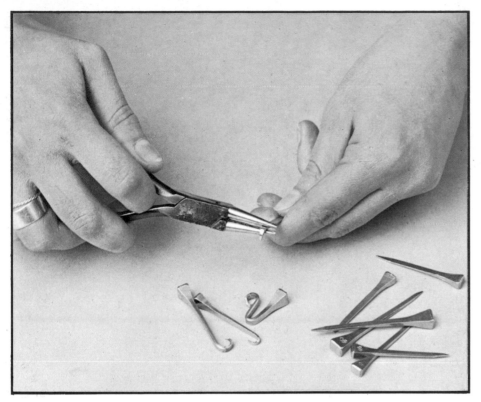

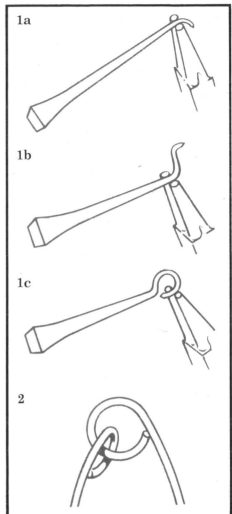

The nails are bent in three stages and this technique forms the basis for all the following horseshoe nail designs.

Note: When working these designs, always keep the trade-mark on the nail on the side to which the end curls.

Start by curling the tip first (fig.1a). Then bend it backwards gently (fig.1b) before completing the curl in the other direction (fig.1c).

Remember to always grip with the pliers in the same position on each nail.

If you can bend the nails without heating them, thread the beads on before bending, but omit the beads if you are heating the nails. Bend the 5 nails in the same manner.

Using the 0.8mm (gauge 20-21) wire, cut 9cm (3½in) to make the horseshoe shape. Shape the wire with your fingers.

From one end thread on 3 red beads, 1 small horseshoe nail, 1 red bead, 1 medium horseshoe nail, 1 red bead, 1 small horseshoe nail and 3 red beads.

Join the 2 ends by making a hook and eye (fig.2).

Make 4 coils of wire, each with 10 'rings' and one jump ring, with a diameter of 5mm (3/16in).

Onto the length of 1.4mm (gauge 15-17) wire, thread 5 red beads,

Above left: Curling the nails using round-nosed pliers.
1a. Curl the front of the nail first.
1b. Second stage in curling.
1c. The end is curled to form an eye.
2. Joining the two ends of the wire.

one coil of wire, one red bead, one medium sized horseshoe nail, one red bead, one coil of wire, one red bead.

Attach the jump ring to the assembled horseshoe shape and thread the jump ring onto the wire.

Thread the remaining beads, coils and nail onto the wire to complete the pattern as for the other side.

Make a hook and eye at each end of the wire to complete the necklace.

The small pendant

The length of the pendant is about 5cm (2in). The length of leather thong attached to the pendant is as required.

Curl the large horseshoe nail used as the centre of the pendant. Bend the nails on each side of the centre nail. Remember to keep the trade-marks on both nails on the outside of the design.

Use the wire to assemble and secure the nails. The wire is tucked in and wrapped over itself on the reverse side. The other end is cut off against the nail and pressed down flat with the pliers.

Bend the medium-sized nail into a U-shape.

The loop on the centre nail of the assembled piece is slipped onto this U-shape. The pointed end of the U-shaped nail is then curled back into a tight curl.

Thread the leather thong through the curl.

Make a jump ring and thread the 2 ends of the thong through the jump ring so that the jump ring keeps the pendant in position in the centre of the thong.

The large pendant

The pendant is 14cm (5½in) long.

Make the hook for the leather thong as for the previous pendant.

Use 5 nails to make the centre piece from which the other nails are suspended. Use the wire to hold them in position.

Attach the hanging nails to each other and to the central piece with jump rings.

Secure the pendant onto the thong with the remaining jump ring.

The large necklace

The length of this necklace can be varied by the number of nails and jump rings used but do not use too many nails or the necklace will be too heavy.

The 3 nails in the centre of the necklace are a large size as are the longer ones along the necklace. The shortest looking nails are medium sized. They are bent into an S-shape with an elongated end. These are combined with jump rings in assembling the necklace.

The small pendant
You will need : Horseshoe nails – one large, one medium and 2 small. 30.5cm (12in) of 0.8mm (gauge 20-21) wire as for the previous necklace. Leather thong sufficiently long to go around an average neck, and tie. One 9mm (⅜in) jump ring. Tools – as for the previous necklace.
The large pendant
You will need : Leather thong. 13 medium sized horseshoe nails. 0.8mm (gauge 20-21) wire, 51cm (20in) long. 11 jump rings 6mm (¼in) in diameter. Tools – as for the previous necklace.

Pasta brooches and necklaces

The pasta in your kitchen cupboard can, of course, be cooked and eaten with a beautiful sauce. But there is another way to look at spaghetti and its relatives – as the raw materials of cheap, bright and original jewelry.

Thanks to Italian culinary inventiveness, there are myriad shapes to choose from. Start with the familiar spaghetti and macaroni, chopped up and arranged in graded lengths for an art deco look, then move onto little rings, shells, wheels and 'occhi di lupo' or wolf's eyes.

Use them singly, arrange them in rows and clusters, paint them in muted or brilliant colours, then fix them with a dab of glue. By combining different colours, by cutting the pasta shapes and arranging them cleverly, it is possible to build up pieces of jewelry that bears no relation to their originally humble and familiar components.

Brooches and pins

Begin by cutting out a base shape from a piece of stiff cardboard. Paint the pasta pieces with poster colours or coloured inks, and finish them off once they are dry with a coat of clear varnish for sparkle. Alternatively, use glossy enamel paints.

When the pasta is dry, check the arrangement on the cardboard base, and then anchor the pieces in position with a suitably strong adhesive.

Finish off the brooch with a suitably-sized jeweler's finding glued to the back of the cardboard.

Necklaces

Tubular pastas make ideal beads. Paint the beads as above and thread them on black shirring elastic thread – choker necklaces can be pulled on over the neck without requiring the extra complication of a clasp.

Other varieties of pasta can also be threaded – with a little care. A hole can be pierced through a shell shape, for example, using a sharp darning needle.

Pasta brooches and necklets

You will need :
Pasta in different shapes and sizes.
Brooch mountings.
Shirring elastic [thread] from necklaces.
Strong adhesive.
Stiff cardboard for base.
Enamel paints, poster paints and varnish.

Above: Hat pin using a more complex arrangement of pasta shapes.
Left: Even the humblest materials can be decorated and then made up into attractive jewelry. The wide variety of unusual pasta shapes available give plenty of scope for making brooches, necklaces and pins.

Far left: Painted to match the dominant colour, this pasta brooch makes an ideal fashion accessory.

Bracelets from forks and spoons

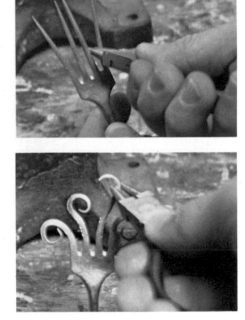

Having flattened the fork prongs with the mallet, the outside prongs are then curled at the base.
Above: Curling the prongs using the round-nosed pliers.

Opposite: Pieces of jewelry made by bending forks. If the plating has worn away, the completed jewelry can be replated by a jeweler or silversmith.

Household spoons and forks are generally considered decorative when they are laid out on a table set for a dinner party. But even then their decorative qualities are taken for granted, or not seen at all. Bracelets and rings are extremely simple to make.

To get started does not mean you have to deplete the kitchen drawer of all its contents. You might have some odd pieces you can practice on, and attractive odds and ends can often be bought cheaply from bric-a-brac shops. If you buy forks make sure that they have handles long enough to bend around the average wrist. Small spoons, such as those used for mustard, can be made into rings. You can use beads and stones from old costume jewelry or you can buy suitable beads from craft stores. The stones can be glued to the jewelry with an epoxy resin adhesive or you can bend the prongs of a fork to hold a stone. However, the jewelry is attractive enough without any added decoration.

The technique for making this kind of jewelry is simple and requires only a little experience before you will be able to produce pieces that appear to be marvellously intricate and skilful.

Fork bracelet

Lay the fork along the flat of the anvil. Use the mallet to flatten the the prongs and neck, but leave the curve at the extreme end of the handle. Make square, light blows to the fork to avoid damaging the surface. Hold the fork with the prongs facing you. Using the round-nosed pliers grip one of the outside prongs and bend it to an angle of about 45°. Repeat with the other outside prong (fig.1). Do not try to force the metal and, above all, do not attempt to bend back to where you started from. Try to keep the positioning of the curves as even as possible. Now start curling the prong from the tip. Make a slight curl to the tip and then keep moving the pliers down along the prong until the curl is complete. Repeat for the other prong. The two inside prongs can now be curled. They can either curl towards each other or away from one another. Start the curl at the tip and work down along the prong as before. If you bend the prongs towards one another, start by bending them away from each other about halfway down their length. Then work from the tip. Check the design and make any adjustment necessary to balance it before proceeding to shape the handle.

Using the mallet start tapping the handle of the fork around the beak of the anvil (or the metal pipe), following the curve, Use square, light blows and move the fork along the beak so that you gradually cover the whole length and then the prongs (fig.2). You can repeat this to get a tighter curve to make a smaller bracelet. Fit the bracelet on an arm and make any adjustments. Polish with metal polish. If your results are good, and the plating has come off the fork, then you can have the bracelet silver-plated by a jeweler. Beads are glued in position when the article is complete.

Alternative designs are easy as you can bend the prongs in various directions, but remember that the simplicity of design combined with the chunky [heavy] quality is appealing in itself.

Fork bracelet

You will need :
Small anvil or else a flat metal surface and a piece of metal pipe.
Mallet – covered with a hide head.
Round-nosed pliers – medium sized will give better results than small ones as spoons and forks can be quite hard to bend, depending on the type of metal.
Vice.
Fork.
Metal polish.

Section tube necklaces

These necklaces are made from clear plastic tubing used for syphoning and as long as the tube ends are well plugged, they can be filled with a multitude of objects.

Section tube necklace

Cut the tube into eight 5cm (2in) pieces. Cut eight pieces of elastic thread 6.5cm (2½in) long.

Thread three large beads on each piece of elastic thread and knot each end to secure beads.

Plug a tube firmly with one of the threaded beads. Hold the tube upright and fill with seed beads to within 6mm (¼in) of tube end (fig.1) then add next bead plug.

Continue this until you have eight tubes filled with beads.

For the final plug you will need a bead with an elastic thread loop. Cut a piece of elastic thread 8cm (3in) long and knot two ends together.

Thread double elastic thread through the bead and make a knot at the base of the loop close to the bead.

String tube on seed bead string

Double thread the needle with thread to the length required and knot one end of nylon thread to the clasp eye. Thread on seed beads to a 20cm (8in) length. Then thread a large bead and put the needle through the tubing. Push a bead into the tube then hold the tube upright and fill tightly with seed beads. Thread a needle through the remaining large bead and push it into the end of the tube.

Continue threading seed beads until the two lengths are equal. Knot thread to the remaining clasp eye.

Glitter plait [braid]

Plug one end of each piece of thin tube with a bugle bead. Make a small paper funnel and pour green glitter into two of the tubes and silver into the third.

When full, plug the remaining ends with bugle beads.

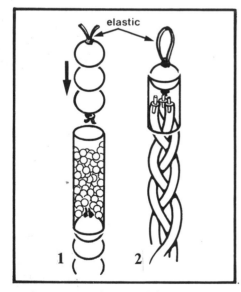

Above: Finishing off the necklaces with a bead plug.

Push three ends of the filled tubes into one piece of large tube. Ask a friend to hold this end and plait [braid] tubes.

When finished, plug remaining three ends in the other piece of large tube (fig.2).

Close the open ends of the large tubes with beads. Knot two beads together with elastic thread for the one tube and make a loop for the other end as for the section tube necklace.

Glitter choker

Knot two beads with elastic thread. Plug one end of the tube with one of the beads. Hold the tube upright and fill with glitter. Plug the other end with a bead and elastic thread loop as for the section tube necklace.

131

Tissue paper jewelry

Twisted tissue jewels are bright and gay – and far more durable than such a fragile paper suggests. They are simple to make and it is fun creating designs. If you wish, of course, you can use purpose-bought tissue to make these boldly beautiful jewel effects. But, providing you have a colourful selection to hand, it is quite unnecessary to buy tissues especially for this craft. Used tissue has the advantage of being cost free and is, in fact, the ideal material, because the techniques involved in making tissue jewels include cutting, tearing, crumpling and twisting the paper.

Basic jewel shapes

There are only two basic jewel shapes – 'stones' and 'strings'. 'Stones,' irrespective of size, are always made by the same method. First a piece of tissue paper is screwed up and rolled between the palms into a ball shape. Wrap the tissue paper ball tightly in a piece of tissue just large enough to encase it completely.

Then cover the ball with a larger piece of tissue. Pinch and twist the ends of this piece of tissue to form a neck, having spread the inside of the neck paper with a little clear general purpose adhesive. When the adhesive has completely dried, snip off the neck with a pair of sharp scissors and slightly flatten the ball in the palm of your hand to give it a domed top and a flattish base. This is to make the stone easier to mount onto the surface to be decorated.

'Strings,' whether long or short, are always made by the same method. It is difficult to make successful 'strings' using strips of tissue over 23cm (9in) in length, but the effect of a longer 'string' can be achieved by butting two or more strings end to end when mounting the jewels.

Cut a piece of tissue to the length required, making it 2.5cm to 6cm (1in to 2½in) wide. Fold the long cut edges neatly towards the centre.

Moisten the forefinger and thumb of both hands with a little water and twist the strip of tissue into a string (fig.6). Work slowly and carefully from one end of the strip to the other always keeping the twisting movement in the same direction.

Right: Making the tissue paper bangle.
1. Measurements for the cardboard bangle must allow for the seam overlap.
2. Hold the glued seam in place with paperclips and leave to dry.
3. Stick the tissue around the bangle and over the top and bottom edges.
4. Draw a thread of glue onto the bangle and stick a 'string' onto it.

To make a bangle

Cut a piece of cardboard 5cm to 7.5cm (2in to 3in) wide and long enough to encompass your hand at the knuckles plus 1cm ($\frac{3}{4}$in) overlap (fig.1).

Mark the overlap on the ends of the cardboard. Then, to join into a circle, spread a thin coat of adhesive on both inner surfaces of the overlap.

When the adhesive is sticky form the strip into a ring, overlapping the glued ends by 2cm ($\frac{3}{4}$in).

Use paper clips to hold the overlap securely and slip the bangle over a bottle to hold it in a circular shape while it dries (fig.2).

When the bangle is completely dry, remove it from the bottle and give a gentle squeeze to form a complete circle.

Now cover the bangle with tissue to provide a colourful background for your jewels. Cut a piece of tissue equal to the circumference and 1.2cm ($\frac{1}{2}$in) wider than the bangle.

Spread the whole outside of the bangle with a thin even coat of adhesive and spread a little adhesive on the inside top edge of the bangle. While the adhesive is still wet, press the tissue paper into position around the bangle, and sticking 6mm ($\frac{1}{4}$in) overlap over the top and inside the bangle (fig.3). Don't worry if a few wrinkles appear in the tissue paper.

Spread a little adhesive along the inside bottom edge of the bangle, and stick down the tissue overlap.

Cut a piece of tissue equal to the circumference of the bangle and

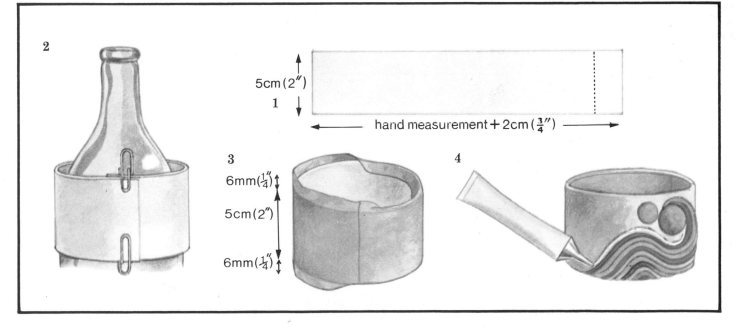

2

5cm (2″)

1

hand measurement + 2cm ($\frac{3}{4}$″)

3

6mm($\frac{1}{4}$″)

5cm (2″)

6mm($\frac{1}{4}$″)

4

fractionally narrower than its width. Spread a thin coat of adhesive over the inside of the bangle and stick the tissue into position while the adhesive is still wet. While the bangle is drying, prepare 'stones' and 'strings' you will need to decorate your bangle (see above).

If you are using 'stones' and 'strings', stick the 'stones' onto the bangle first. Spread the underside of the stone thinly with adhesive and, when sticky, press firmly into position on the bangle.

'Strings' may need to be re-rolled before gluing. Quickly re-twist them into shape. Don't apply adhesive to the 'string' but apply a thin thread of it to the bangle, drawing the thread in the desired pattern (fig.4).

Then press the 'string' into position along the glue line. Use tweezers if required to help position the 'string'.

When the bejeweled bangle is quite dry, spray inside and out with clear varnish. Spray lightly (the dyes in tissue are inclined to run if the paper gets very wet) and when dry, give a second coat.

For greater durability later, add a third coat of varnish.

Right: The finished bangle and matching bird brooch. Tissue jewelry is ideal for making props for children's plays and is surprisingly durable when varnished.

Index

Picture Credits

Theo Bergstrom p.38/9, 121, 129
Steve Bicknell p.8, 19, 26, 28/9, 30, 32, 42, 43,
    52, 56B, 57, 58, 73, 76, 103
Colorific/David Moore p.93
Stuart Dalby p.128
Alan Duns p.98, 100
Melvin Grey 11, 111, 112, BL
Peter Heinz p.6, 120, 122
Geoff Howes p.107
100 Ideas/Liddell p.35, Capurro p.47, Dirand
    p.126, 127
Paul Kemp p.91, 101, 106
Chris Lewis p.5, 13, 15, 124
Sandra Lousada p.17, 69, 80
Dick Miller p.20/1, 54, 63BL, 82, 108R, 109,
    114, 123
Jane Morris p.41, 46
Keith Morris p.116
Tony Moussoulides p.24

Walter Murray p.79
Alasdair Ogilvie p.7, 10, 70, 131
Roger Payling p.118
Roger Phillips p.117
Peter Pugh-Cook p.49
Kim Sayer p.31, 34, 45, 95/6, 97
Syndication International/Womancraft p.84/5
Jerry Tubby p.60, 134
Mike van der Vord p.62, 63BR

Artwork :

Kay Designs p.23T, B
Victoria Drew p.28, 36/7, 56L, 57R
Barbara Firth p.133
John Hutchinson p.51
Coral Mula p.30
Jacqueline Short p.21R, 22, 23M
Trevor Lawrence p.58B, 70, 123, 130
Paul Williams p.17, 18, 59, 61, 62, 63T, 75, 78,
    84, 86, 87, 88, 90, 105, 108, 110, 112
Anne Winterbottom p.9, 10